The Hidden Curriculum of Online Learning

Challenging the current understandings of equity and social justice in the field of online education, *The Hidden Curriculum of Online Learning* analyses how cultural hegemony creates unfair learning experiences through cultural differences. It argues that such inequitable learning experiences are not random acts but rather represent the existing inequities in society at large through cultural reproduction.

Based on an ethnographic work, the book discusses the concept of social absence (in relation to social presence) to discuss how individuals perform their identities within group contexts and to create awareness of social justice issues in online education. It draws upon critical pedagogy and cultural studies to show that while online learning spaces are frequently promoted by local or federal governments and higher education institutions as overwhelmingly inclusive and democratic, these premises do not operate with uniformity across all student cohorts.

The Hidden Curriculum of Online Learning will be of great interest to academics, post-graduate students, and researchers in the fields of digital learning and inclusion, education research, and cultural studies.

Murat Öztok is a Lecturer in the Department of Educational Research at Lancaster University, UK.

Perspectives on Education in the Digital Age
Series Editors: David Kergel and Birte Heidkamp

The process of digitalization is leading to a fundamental social change affecting all spheres of social life. In the pedagogical field there is a need for re-structuring key concepts such as learning, teaching and education that considers socio-economic and cultural changes.

Perspectives on Education in the Digital Age explores the process of coming to terms with socio-economic and socio-cultural shifts arising from digitalization and discusses this process with reference to its effects on education. The Series provides a forum for discussion of critical, integrative analyses of social transformations in the digital age, drawn from different fields such as the humanities, social sciences and economics. The aim of the Series is to analyse the implications of cultural change on education in the digital age by bringing together interdisciplinary dialogue and different theoretical approaches.

The Hidden Curriculum of Online Learning
Understanding Social Justice through Critical Pedagogy
Murat Öztok

The Hidden Curriculum of Online Learning

Understanding Social Justice through Critical Pedagogy

Murat Öztok

LONDON AND NEW YORK

First published 2020
by Routledge
2 Park Square, Milton Park, Abingdon, Oxon, OX14 4RN

and by Routledge
52 Vanderbilt Avenue, New York, NY 10017

Routledge is an imprint of the Taylor & Francis Group, an informa business

First issued in paperback 2021

© 2020 Murat Öztok

The right of Murat Öztok to be identified as authors of this work has been asserted by him in accordance with sections 77 and 78 of the Copyright, Designs and Patents Act 1988.

All rights reserved. No part of this book may be reprinted or reproduced or utilised in any form or by any electronic, mechanical, or other means, now known or hereafter invented, including photocopying and recording, or in any information storage or retrieval system, without permission in writing from the publishers.

Trademark notice: Product or corporate names may be trademarks or registered trademarks, and are used only for identification and explanation without intent to infringe.

British Library Cataloguing-in-Publication Data
A catalogue record for this book is available from the British Library

Library of Congress Cataloging-in-Publication Data
A catalog record for this book has been requested

ISBN: 978-0-367-24715-7 (hbk)
ISBN: 978-1-03-209059-7 (pbk)
ISBN: 978-0-429-28405-2 (ebk)

Typeset in Bembo
by Apex CoVantage, LLC

Babam için

Contents

Preface		viii
Acknowledgements		xi
1	Genealogy of the concepts and the myths of equity in online learning	1
2	How to study equity in online spaces: situating the theoretical frameworks	17
3	Writing oneself into online being: the art of self-representation and impression management	37
4	Hierarchy of privilege: self as curriculum of diversity and otherness	57
5	Sociocultural production of self: social presence and social absence	83
6	Hidden curriculum of online learning: Discourses of whiteness, social absence, and inequity	106
	Index	114

Preface

My journey that led me to write this book was as exciting as it was challenging. Studying and working at one of the oldest, biggest, and most diverse institutions in Canada was a privilege I tremendously enjoyed – not least because I benefited from all its academic rigour and opportunities it provided but also because I felt I am accepted and welcomed as who I am in that *multicultural* institution. Indeed, multiculturalism was recognised by the Canadian Bill of Rights in 1982 and became a law by the Canadian Multiculturalism Act in 1988. It was a promise that the Government of Canada would recognise and respect its society including its diversity in languages, customs, religions, and so on. The ideas and questions that shaped this book were born out of my experience to understand who I am in this multicultural country and in this multicultural institution.

Before I started my PhD education, I was a teacher with a background in computer science and psychology. Theories of whiteness, post-colonial approaches, the concept of cultural hegemony, and other critical concepts I employed in this book were alien to me. Whilst the course I took during my doctoral study were loaded with such perspectives, none of them made perfect sense to me until I started to wonder about who I am and how I am positioned in relation to my peers when one of my classmates told me I could pretend to be a Canadian because I was white enough but I had to keep my mouth closed (because I did not have a Canadian accent). This otherwise offensive – and unnecessary – comment coming from a friend was an intellectual catharsis by which I started to make sense of critical pedagogy. I realised that I was the subject of a story that was similar to the stories or examples I have been studying in the writings of Cheryl Harris or Peggy McIntosh. The rest of my time in Canada – and in the USA afterwards and currently in the United Kingdom – has been a continuous struggle and renegotiation of my identify in relation to the notions of whiteness and white privilege – or white ignorance for that matter.

After this intellectually cathartic moment, the way I make sense of myself as a demographically but not culturally white person soon expanded itself to my research main interest: online education. As I have argued throughout in this book, I subscribe to the argument that online and offline spaces are not dichotomous entities nor can they be conceptualised without one another. Then, did my peers in online courses I participated in think the same of me? What did it mean to be white in online spaces anyway? Was I going crazy about how to make sense of myself or perhaps going through an identity crisis in the form of a psychological trauma; or, were there others who were experiencing similar struggles? As a curious PhD student, I wanted to read more about the applications of critical pedagogy in online education in order to find some answers, but it was not a surprise to me that I was not able to find any significant work. The lack of critical perspectives in online education research, particularly the lack of post-colonial approaches and the analysis of whiteness, opened up a new research interest to me that defined my career so far as a scholar.

In this book, I try to understand ways of being online by questioning it in the intersection of power and agency. I invite the readers to explore how social, historical, economic, and political analysis can materialise the social fabric in online spaces. It is through this analysis that we can actually question the discourses that traditionally define the theory and practice of online education, and the broader field of educational research. We need to look at online education from a different lens, one which raises new questions and requires new formulations. How do we understand the relationship between subjectivity and education? How are the oppressive forms of power created in online spaces? Who are we and how do we situate ourselves in relation to such oppressive forms of power? This book does not provide a blueprint for such questions, but it opens up a discussion for grappling with them.

This book is situated within my own intellectual, cultural, and personal experience with online education. As I have explained in great detail in Chapter 2, I refused the safety of established theoretical perspectives employed in online education, challenged the determinism of discourses that defined online education, and went against the cynicism that relegated people in online spaces to a place outside of power struggle. This was necessary because online education was branded as a remedy for the widening intellectual, economic, social, and political gaps among different cohorts of students. Online education was championed for its capacity to democratise educational systems by acting as the great equaliser. The rhetoric concerning the centrality of online education for democratic transformation was grounded in the widespread belief that online spaces can provide any time anywhere access. However, it is much too facile simply to argue that providing access to people is good enough for ensuring social justice in any given educational system. Even though the questions that researchers ask concerning social justice are becoming more precise, and the methods used in undertaking research are getting increasingly sophisticated, there is a dearth of theoretical frameworks for conceptualising social justice in online education.

Online education research has long focused on what to teach, how to teach, how to design teaching activities; researchers have long questioned how knowledge is cultivated in and utilised through collaboration, how people interact with and react to one another during group work. Indeed, there is no doubt that these accounts have provided us much needed information for excelling at teaching and learning in online spaces. On the contrary, not much research has engaged with questions concerning what it means to *be* in an online space. The relationship between who we are (or who we become) in online spaces and how we engage with each other (or engage with teaching and learning materials) is relatively unknown. This book aims to set a new standard for engaging with the problems and possibilities of online education. The first chapter of the book introduces the current state of online education with respect to the theories of social justice. In order to illustrate, situate, and contextualise why and how critical perspectives are largely ignored, I trace down the origins and the historical development of online education. In the second chapter, I explain in detail how to conceptualise social justice in online spaces. This chapter draws from the concepts in, approaches to, and frameworks for social justice from a broad range of disciplines. The keys to this chapter are the questions concerning *being* online. Chapters 3, 4, and 5 put these theories and approaches in action and show how everyday discourses operate to produce differentiated learning experiences. In particular, while Chapter 3 explores how *online selves* are created as a dynamic play of impression management, Chapter 4 shows that online selves are the mechanism by which social hierarchy is created and maintained. Chapter 5 provides a pedagogical analysis of this social hierarchy. The last chapter, Chapter 6, brings all these accounts together in order to demonstrate the ways in which societal discourses create social hegemony against those who fall outside the ideations of white perspectives. Taken all the chapters together, this book aims to cast some light on this process.

I do hope that scholars, researchers, teachers, students, administrators, and those who like to engage with the complex sociocultural and ideological landscapes will find this book a useful resource, one that provides a cautionary argument against the fairy tale stories of online education. This is important because whilst online education is overwhelmingly promoted as inclusive and democratic, these premises do not operate with uniformity across all student cohorts, particularly in an age of growing student diversity. Yet, local and federal governments, public school boards, and higher education institutions have been promoting online education in their commitment to accommodating public needs, widening access to education, sharing intellectual resources, and reducing costs without much considering the ways in which discursive elements inherent in online education operate to marginalise students who fall outside ideations of dominant discourses. We need to reconsider what online education *is* and *does*; we need to understand people and their experiences. We need to consider the hidden curriculum of online education.

Acknowledgements

Many have influenced me and helped me, and I want to acknowledge those who contributed to this work with their thoughts, insights, and feelings.

I want to start with Professor Clare Brett. Without her support and encouragement, I would not be able to explore the critical educational theory in online education. Our conversations have greatly helped me to connect the missing dots between critical theories and teaching/learning in online spaces. Professor Indigo Esmonde and Professor Ruben Gaztambide-Fernandez have been invaluable to me. Indigo and Ruben were demanding critics. Without their exhaustive comments and suggestions in the earlier versions of this work I could not be able to turn my loose ideas into a coherent body of arguments. Ruben and Indigo were my compass when I thought I was lost in the terrain of critical educational theory. Professor Jim Hewitt was an intellectual resource to me; his careful comments have helped me to situate my work into the field of online education.

My conversations with my colleagues have helped and encouraged me, and I learned a great deal from them. Dr. Kyungmee Lee has been very helpful to me; we spent many hours and enjoyed pints of beer discussing various topics, from critical theories of education to critical theories of technology. Dr. Daniel Zingaro has been the most influential and helpful during this work. We spent countless hours discussing academic topics while we were playing computer games and discussing strategies to defeat our virtual nemeses. I cannot list all the things that I have learned from him but, for sure, I have learned great deal from him.

I would also like to thank to my participants, who not only welcomed me in their online courses but also committed time and shared their insights and feelings with me. Without their assistance and support, this work would not be possible.

Chapter 1

Genealogy of the concepts and the myths of equity in online learning

Learning is simultaneously an individual and cultural process. It is the material, symbolic, and intellectual reconstruction of self, a process of discovering and articulating oneself in relation to others. In other words, it is a process of knowing the self through mediation between self and others (Pinar, 2004). What mediates between the self and the others – between the personal and cultural – is referred to as subjectivity. Thus, the process of education is the process of constructing and shaping individuals' subjectivity, consciously or unconsciously (Greene, 1971).

In the field of online education, subjectivity is understood and studied through the concept of social presence (Oztok & Kehrwald, 2017); that is, the degree to which individuals represent themselves and perceive others in online spaces. Much research has argued that a sense of social presence plays a significant role in an online learning community (Oztok & Brett, 2011). While the documented benefits of social presence may hold some truth, such perspectives solely focus on the positive aspects of community but ignore the implicit ways in which group work may perpetuate inequity. A positive sense of community and productive group work cannot be expected for every individual under every circumstance. Indeed, scholars have noted that when not implemented carefully, group work in learning communities may aggravate equity issues (Esmonde, 2009). That is, individuals can feel that they are consistently or systematically marginalised, isolated, devalued, or even oppressed in a group work setting. Consequently, in order to work towards more equitable learning conditions in online education, it is important to understand how individuals perceive their online subjectivities and experience the curriculum of online education.

Understanding whether a given learning practice, context, or work is equitable is not straightforward. Because equity is a value-laden term and requires human judgement of whether the given circumstances are just or fair, what equity might empirically mean is contingent on the context and open to debate. That is, equity might mean different things for different individuals under different circumstances. Indeed, there is no widely agreed-upon definition of the concept nor is there a widely agreed-upon understanding of how we might identify or address it. Nevertheless, the ways in which equity is defined have implications for how equity concerns are addressed.

2 Genealogy of concepts and myths of equity

Current research on equity argues for a distinction between equity and equality. While equity refers to justice or fairness in a given situation, equality means sameness (Esmonde, 2009). In terms of education specifically, equity focuses on the qualitative judgement of the learning situation or the learning process while equality is concerned with the quantitative measurement of educational inputs, treatment, or outputs. Based on this distinction, equity judgements should go beyond the issues of equal access or equal treatment and consider how social, political, and historical dynamics can create unfair or unjust learning situations. In order to frame what constitutes equity, we should move beyond investigating patterns of courses taken by various race groups or genders (i.e. white students do this, black students do that), and instead consider the cultural processes by which inequity is continuously created and maintained. According to this perspective, equity is not a static outcome of certain treatments of certain groups or individuals; rather, it is a process that is situated between the tensions of various social structures that exist in cultural settings. Fundamental to my perspective is the idea that equity is not about providing a point of sameness among individuals, but about enabling them to become agents of their own learning by appropriating the learning repertoires they need in order to fulfil their potential. Conceptualising equity in relation to sociocultural dynamics and hegemony, of course, invites a discussion about the process by which subjectivities are defined and developed.

Consequently, this book analyses how material realities of daily life impose the dominant perspectives on individuals' identification and operate to produce unfair learning contexts. I demonstrate how and why online learning research has failed to conceptualise equity in relation to Discourses[1] on the one hand and learning conditions on the other. In what follows, I turn to the historical trajectory of educational technology in order to understand the theories and concepts in which the current perspectives and traditions in online education are grounded. I analyse the historical development of education in and through the use of online spaces in relation to the socio-historical conditions under which general education and public schooling are transformed. Tracing the broader Discourses that subjugate the educational policies, theories, and practices, I change the emphasis from *how* technology is used to *why* technology is used. By doing so, this book addresses equity as fundamentally tied to societal Discourses inherent in education and schooling, contextualising online education within the broader societal struggle among different groups over questions regarding the purpose of schooling, how children learn, whose knowledge is to be legitimated, and what social relations would prevail.

When education in general and schooling in particular is considered, the relationship between technology and learning can be thought of as a post-Fordist project, driven by neo-liberalism (Kliebard, 1986). While economic and political concerns have always been central to the debates regarding education and schooling, efficiency and accountability models for curriculum have influenced the theory and practice of education since the post-Sputnik era (Apple, 2004). The industrial revolution produced its own cultural beliefs in science and technology, and it was a time of an emerging positivism when scientific techniques were finding their way into educational theory and practice through the marriage of science and technology. The industrialisation turned schools into technical training institutions, where students were educated to meet the national standards in literacy, math, and science (Aronowitz & Giroux, 1991). In order to correspond with such demands in schooling and education, school boards, educational institutions, and governmental agencies turned to technology since technology was believed to be effective[2] for training mass amounts of American soldiers in a short period of time during the Second World War (Seattler, 2004).

Sociopolitical Discourses, therefore, promoted automation of teaching, arguing that replacing faculty with technological instructional products (e.g., CDs, videos, computer software) would address the fiscal concerns regarding public schools. The concepts of efficiency and productivity[3] formed the theory and practice of educational technology, defining the field as a modernist project (Trend, 2001). Educational use of technology as a research field developed out of the concerns for cost-effectiveness in education and schooling. Educational technology scholars have conceptualised pedagogy in terms of transmission of academic content knowledge, reproducibility of pedagogical materials, and efficiency of teaching and learning activities but have largely ignored pedagogy as a deliberate and critical attempt to influence the ways in which knowledge and identities are produced within and among particular sets of social relations. Much of the educational technology research can be described as the study of *instructional science* – a work that is concerned with the role of technology in using teaching and learning materials. Consequently, the theory and practice of research regarding the educational uses of technology have tended to explore either supporting the development of learning spaces, or else enhancing the use of learning materials (Selwyn, 2010). The curriculum of educational technology, then, is predominantly accepted as something an instructor does to implement a pre-constituted body of knowledge and is therefore improvable by increasingly complex applications of technology.

The same arguments, to a great extent, can be applied to the theory and practice of online education. While there is no single evolutionary point from which online education originated academically, many scholars suggest that it emerged around the 1980s when practices of educational technology were integrated with distance learning (although there is no clear distinction between distance education and online education, distance education practices can be traced back to educational radio, or even the earlier practices of educational mail) (Ely, 1999). The implications of this are largely manifest in the practice of online education. What to teach and how to teach continue to dominate the questions concerning teaching and learning activities. Pedagogical discussions

4 Genealogy of concepts and myths of equity

and debates are limited with deciding the content and scope of topics/subjects to teach, methods or strategies to implement pedagogical activities, instructional materials to deliver these knowledge, skills, and/or attitudes (Kanuka, 2008).

Taken together, it is possible to strongly argue that, in accord with Tyler's (1949) rationale of curriculum, many online education scholars have been concerned with deciding and conveying the academic content and the skills that students are expected to gain but have disregarded the social structures of the broader context. Positivist and post-Fordist pedagogical guidelines have limited the scope of online education. Research has addressed students as a unified body and argued that learning in online spaces transcends culture, disregarding the struggle over meanings and practices. Ignoring how schools operate as agencies of social and cultural reproduction, online education research has ignored the ways in which various social, economic, and political interests bear down on and shape the day-to-day practices of classroom life. This is evident in the current state of theory and practice of online education. Frameworks for, perspectives in, and approaches to participation, collaboration, and equity inherently ignore the societal dynamics, power struggles, and ideologies.

Technological determinism is the ultimate concept at the intersection of these liberal, positivist, and post-Fordist Discourses that have been shaping the theory and practice of online education. Within the deterministic framework, the concepts of affordability and cost-effectiveness can serve as a selection criterion for determining successful and failed applications of technology (Feenberg, 2002). In its simplest definition, technological determinism refers to the philosophical stance that technology is the driving force in the modern world. The idea that technology is the sole changing force can be traced back to the concept's etymology: in Greek, *techné* can be understood as the craft-based approach to producing or achieving something and it is often discussed in terms of the systematic application of science (or scientific knowledge) to control or alter the nature for human's needs or desires (Heidegger, 1977). It suggests that technology is an external and autonomous force that is independent of the context in which it is used and is exempt from the complex interplay of historical, social, economic, and political forces. According to this perspective, technology defines the rules and conditions for social formation as it affects our cognition and influences our sensorium, which in return determines our social behaviour and defines our culture. Thus, proponents of this perspective argue that technology's effects are not bounded by the processes in which it is used.

Opponents of this perspective argue that technology is value free and has no inherent qualities. However, this approach disregards the potentials and affordances that technology offers. Rather than thinking of technology as an external force shaping society or an irrelevant actor in it, this book adopts a point of balance between these two perspectives in order to go beyond the notion of technology as a simple *cause* of social change on the one hand and the idea of technology as an easy *fix* for complex social problems on the other (Buckingham, 2008). In this dialectical approach, technology is another dimension among various societal factors (Feenberg, 2002). That is, while technology has its own inherent constraints and possibilities to affect social life, its production, use, and distribution is shaped and appropriated by social actors and institutions. Technology comes with its own materiality. It enables certain ways to function and provides virtually limitless possibilities while simultaneously being subject to Discourses of the cultural context in which it is being employed. Such a conceptualisation provides better means to understand the larger economic, political, and cultural dynamics behind the use of technology – and thus behind online spaces.

Frankfurt School[4] theorists have arguably provided the most influential accounts regarding technology and its sociocultural implications in daily life. Specifically, analysing the effects of technology in both the production and consumption of mass cultural goods, Frankfurt School theorists documented how mass media uses subtle means of control and creates tyranny by changing the experience and perceptions of individuals (Adorno, 2001). They argued that mass media manipulates people into a state of pessimism, and thus instrumentality can lead to oppression as it induces the foundation of social domination over individuality and free will. Although the Frankfurt School theorists mainly criticised the culture industry[5] by exploring the implications of mass production of cultural goods, their perspective on the effects of technology inspired scholars across the globe. Employing the deterministic view of technology, many influential media theorists and scholars studied the effects of technology on culture and society. For instance, media scholars employing this perspective have argued that social power structures are conveyed through the dominant forms of media tools and that changes in the dominant medium alter individuals' world views and create biases through which a society's orientation and values are shaped (McLuhan, 1964).

In the case of education, the deterministic view of technology influenced the curriculum of educational technology, shaping the classroom activities and the pedagogical practices by which technology is used. Stemming from this techno-romantic perspective, the de facto role of the educational technologist was to *harness the power of technology* by finding ways to fix or enhance teaching and learning situations with technology-based improvements (Selwyn, 2010). This is what the Frankfurt School theorists call instrumental rationality. It represents the de-socialised view of technology by ignoring various Discourses behind the relation of technology to education, curriculum, and pedagogy. Thus, it reduces the importance of human agency by suggesting that technology itself defines the ways in which individuals engage with each other in online spaces.

In order to understand how these deterministic perspectives play a role particularly in online education, I analyse the current conceptualisations of online education in two categories: (1) open-flexible access, which leads scholars to suggest that individuals can access online materials or spaces anytime and anywhere, and thus that online learning spaces provide and sustain equity; and

6 Genealogy of concepts and myths of equity

(2) a neutral space, which leads scholars to suggest that mediated spaces are inherently culturally value free, and thus individuals in these spaces are, by extension, assumed to be equal.

1.1 Open-flexible access

Open-flexible access refers to the capacities of online education technology that provide flexible and increased access to educational resources. This perspective supports an anywhere, anytime view of online spaces as it is concerned with the issues of access to educational resources. Questions concerning open-flexible access are heavily influenced by liberalism; therefore, scholars employing this conceptual mindset have typically emphasised that technology can provide equal educational opportunities for participation, negotiation, and engagement. Proponents of open-flexible access have advocated that the online space is a more democratic and inclusive space compared to typical face-to-face classrooms since technology enables many-to-many communication among peers, facilitates collaborative work, and allows knowledge production regardless of time and space (Harasim, 2000).

Such claims, however, are built on the assumption that digital technology can provide better and enhanced opportunities for more individuals to participate, as if equity and social justice were direct consequences of open-flexible access to the online space. The basic premise of this rhetoric is that the elimination of exclusion as a function of time and place holds the promise of equity. While I acknowledge that open and flexible access is a very worthwhile educational goal, it is important to recognise that having equal access to educational resources affords equality rather than equity. As argued in detail in the next chapter, while equity refers to a contextual judgement of whether the given situation is in line with community ideals of justice, equality refers to quantitative measurements of equal treatment or outcomes.

The open-flexible access perspective has led to two separate yet related research strands: research focused on improving access to online spaces and research focused on improving participation in online spaces.

When issues of access are considered, research has typically focused on the possibilities that technology can afford and has argued that asynchronous computer-mediated communication (CMC) provides ideal conditions for non-dominative, liberal discourses "because everyone can be given [an] equal opportunity to enter arguments in the conference" (Boyd, 1996, p. 181). Building on these early claims, researchers have suggested that online spaces provide open, non-hierarchical, and emancipatory communication among the participants, allowing participants to contribute to discussion from anywhere in the world at any time of the day, with many-to-many interactivity (Harasim, 2000). Typifying the research concerned with access to the online spaces, these early accounts focus on online spaces' effects on temporal and spatial barriers as a condition for equitable learning conditions. Open-flexible access perspectives, therefore, proclaim that technology, by its very nature, opens up possibilities for widening access to higher education; thus, it promotes social equity.

By and large, the current research in online education echoes these early claims as scholars posit that online spaces are free from the limitations of space and time. Online learning spaces are assumed to provide equitable learning conditions based on the opportunities they provide to overcome the *tyranny of space/time* by allowing those who otherwise cannot participate in discussion. In particular, when issues of participation are considered, seemingly equal conversational relations are confused with the presence of equitable learning conditions. Measuring the quantity of messages posted or received, research has concluded that the nature of communication in online spaces provides equitable learning conditions compared to face-to-face discussions since those who are traditionally shut out of discussions – people from various cultural groups, women, minorities, or even people shy in nature – can benefit from the increased possibilities for participation. Focusing on the equality of participation, the literature posits that students from different cultural groups participate equally, that women are as active as men when proposing a solution to a problem, and that those of lower and higher socio-economic status contribute equally to discussion (Bates, 2005).

These studies point out the fact that research concerned with the implications of open-flexible access has addressed educational implications using quantitative outcomes, dropout rates, attendance, or achievement gaps. Simply, the literature has assumed that social equity can be reached to the extent that the digital gap is closed; therefore, it has considered the digital divide as a means to study equity (Warschauer & Matuchniak, 2010). However, equal access can only be a necessary but insufficient premise for equitable learning conditions. That is, just because students can log in to the online space and interact with others does not ensure that there will be equity in their learning experiences. Disregarding the effects of the macro-level Discourses on micro-level classroom practices, research that put open-flexible access to the fore does not address power relationships, otherness, privilege, or marginalisation in relation to the material and symbolic conditions within which the daily learning practices are embedded. As argued in detail in the next chapter, understanding equity in online spaces should go beyond the limited notion of access and include the rules of engagement and the process of identification in learning contexts.

1.2 Neutral space

The notion of neutral space refers to the belief that online spaces erase sociocultural differences. This perspective has led online learning scholars to assume that individuals in online spaces are socially equal by nature. Emphasising the relative anonymity that CMC provides, research has suggested that online spaces provide opportunities for increasing communication among participants and are therefore preferred to typical face-to-face classrooms (Walther, 1996).

8 Genealogy of concepts and myths of equity

Neutrality claims are largely influenced by Habermas's (1984) theory of communicative action.[6] According to this theory, technology is means of modernity and it provides opportunities for individuals to coordinate their actions in the sphere of everyday life. Though Habermas suggested that communicative actions through media can liberate or dominate (or both) different people under different circumstances, online education research has preferentially adapted the liberation perspectives to address the nature of communication among participants. Grounded in such perspectives, the online education literature has suggested that the online space is simply a medium to deliver teaching and learning materials and support pedagogical activities. It does not affect students "any more than the truck that delivers our groceries causes changes in our nutrition" (Clark, 1983, p. 445). Indeed, early online education research has conceptualised communicative actions as mere exchanges, wherein social status cues (sociocultural makeups, accent, appearance, etc.) that might otherwise play a role in face-to-face settings are irrelevant. The lack of social cues is presumed to provide possibility for traditionally lower-status individuals to participate in the teaching and learning activities on the same terms as others. This relative anonymity served as the basis for the presumptions that online spaces can break down social, economic, historical, and political barriers for cultivating and utilising knowledge equally across different cohorts of students.

While current online education research no longer emphasises the loss of sociocultural markers – since the capacity of current technology conveys such information easily – the claims of neutrality continue to influence the discussion regarding the nature of the social fabric in online spaces. The current research suggests that neutrality of the online learning context provides greater learning outcomes compared to face-to-face settings. Such arguments revolve around the notion of disembodiment in online spaces, where in the range of physical clues often associated with face-to-face communication disappear and people adopt a range of personal presentations without the usual aesthetic and tonal limitations imposed by face-to-face verbal communication (Freeman & Bamford, 2004). And, since the neutrality of online spaces is assumed to provide a range of opportunities for participation, many researchers reported that online discussions are more equitable and more democratic than traditional classroom discussions. The current perspectives, therefore, echo the earlier accounts as they suggest that the online space by itself can provide better equitable learning opportunities for facilitation, argumentation, and group work (Swan & Shih, 2005).

However, these perspectives disregard the role of Discourses and their effect on the rules of engagement and the process of identification. They dismiss human agency through the implicit assumption that actions are performed in ways independent from context. Focusing on the affordances of technology while disregarding the sociocultural Discourses leads to the assumption that the online space is a *tabula rasa* and exists without social, cultural, or political origins or assumptions. However, social context is far from neutral and has to be considered in relation to broader dynamics in society. Characteristics such as race, class, sexual orientation, ethnicity, nationality, and gender are the very markers used in society to determine the material and symbolic boundaries and relations. Ignoring these characteristics would be to deny that online space is socially constructed by its inhabitants and constituted by their characteristics.

1.3 Current state of research in online education and challenges

The genealogy of online education suggests that its modernist, positivist, and neo-liberal foundations can be explained as "instructional industrialism" (Evans, 1995); that is, the use of technology only for the purpose of reaching immediate ends, even if these immediate ends are realised through the use of a reductionist curriculum. This instructional industrialism is manifest in the theory and practice of online education: while the notion of neutral space decontextualises the context (disregarding macro-level Discourses), the notion of open-flexible access decontextualises learning practices (disregarding micro-level learning practices). Indeed, when the claims of open-flexible access and neutral space are taken together, the literature concludes that online education can enable conditions for "ideal discourse" (Habermas, 1984), where all participants can contribute equally to the discussion since there are no cues to reflect social status or power relations.

Building upon these accounts, the current state of online education provides idealistic, depoliticised, and normalised perspectives regarding equity in online learning spaces. Online learning research continues to oversimplify human experience by ignoring the ways in which the process of identification and the rules of engagement are produced, contested, and legitimised within the dynamics of everyday life. This normative perspective assumes that identities are given, fixed, or predefined; it tends to generalise the members of a particular group and assimilate them into a singular identity. This reductionist approach works best with Hofstede's (1997) conceptualisation of identification, which defines and categorises individuals through binary terms (i.e. collectivist–individualist, high uncertainty–low uncertainty, or high power–low power). This theory is developed to examine the results of a worldwide survey of employee values by IBM in the 1960s and 1970s. The theory was one of the first that quantified people's characteristics or demographics in order to explain observed differences between cultural groups. Hofstede's taxonomy classifies countries or regions through the aforementioned binary terms and indicates what reactions are likely given one's cultural background. For instance, if a person is identified with individualism based on his or her cultural background, that person is assumed to participate less in group work since individualism pertains to societies in which the ties between individuals are loose: everyone is expected to look after himself or herself and his or her immediate family. On the contrary, a person is believed to be a good collaborator when he or she is identified with collectivism, since collectivism pertains to societies in which people from birth onwards are integrated into strong, cohesive in-groups, which throughout people's lifetime continue to protect them in exchange for unquestioning loyalty (Hofstede, 1997).

This framework can be found in much online learning research. For instance, when research argues that online courses benefit a wide variety of students, but perhaps none more dramatically than non-traditional female students (Sullivan, 2001), it not only suggests that there are enough commonalities among non-traditional female students to allow this analysis to be made but also implies that there is a predefined way to be a female (or a way to be a non-traditional female) in online spaces. The underlying theoretical assumption is that gender categories are predefined, given, and static and that such gender categories are meaningful on their own to explain certain online learning practices. Similarly, when researchers suggest that black students have a significantly weaker sense of community compared to their white peers in an online course (Rovai & Ponton, 2005), it implies that the category of race itself is sufficiently meaningful to inform the understanding of different societal factors that might contribute to a sense of belonging. As it would be a mistake to suggest that whites are more friendly or open for communication than black students, it seems clear that race alone cannot explain this apparent finding. Similar online learning studies making such claims include but are not limited to: a cross-cultural study of social interaction behaviours among Korean, American, and Finnish students (Kim & Bonk, 2006), a quantitative comparison of online learning experience between US and non-US students (Bently & Tinney, 2003); an exploration of success in online learning spaces with respect to people's cultural background (Mills, Eyre, & Harvey, 2005), and an investigation of pedagogical differences between Chinese and Western students (Ku, Pan, Tsai, Tao, & Cornell, 2004). While these studies represent a small slice of research employing Hofstede's normative perspective, they typify the work studying identification, engagement, and group work in relation to the ways that different cultural groups interact with each other.

Research conceptualising the process of identification as a predefined cultural practice based on one's cultural background can summarise the current state of research in online education. However, as this book argues, understanding the relationship between culture at large and education in general starts with understanding culture as the production and legitimation of particular ways of life specific to class, gender, and race. Culture is neither an end in itself nor the product of autonomous agents; instead, it comprises the ongoing contingent Discourses that form how we act, think, and live (Foucault, 1972). Scholars have long investigated the implications of culture and argued that the culture transmitted by the school is related to the various cultures that make up the wider society and that it confirms and sustains the culture of dominant groups while marginalising and silencing the cultures of subordinate groups of students (Giroux, 2011). By disregarding the dynamic interplay between

Discourses and everyday practices of individuals, online education research is unable to acknowledge the complex societal dynamics that structure day-to-day school life. It provides inconclusive arguments – if not wishful imaginations – regarding equitable learning conditions in online spaces.

1.4 Self as an instrument

One's social position affects one's perspectives and the ardour of one's subscription to the values that are socially produced and promoted. In order to explain and justify my position as a researcher and an author, I shall articulate how my perspectives have guided me in problematising the effects of Discourses in online education. Below, I explain how this book has grown around my experience with online learning.

I was an international student in a Canadian research university, being bombarded with the Discourses of multiculturalism: that cultural diversity is protected and promoted to enrich and strengthen Canadian society. Indeed, Canada is among the first countries to adopt a multicultural policy. As good and promising as this sounds, the obscurity surrounding the definition of the term and the murky applications of it as a national policy never matched the promises of well-being it aimed to provide. In fact, many scholars have argued Canada's approach to multiculturalism emerged as a solution to the tension between Franco and Anglo colonial powers around the "Quebec question" (Bannerji, 2000). However, Canada is not the only nation to appropriate the use of multiculturalism to serve its needs. The concept of multiculturalism has always been part of a political agenda around the world. For example, in the United States, multiculturalism evolved in response to the demands of the Civil Rights movement whereas in the United Kingdom, public discussion around multiculturalism started in the post-Second World War era, largely precipitated by the labour migration from its Overseas Territories. By the 1980s, multiculturalism became a scapegoat for the shrinking economy, diminishing public services, and declining personal wealth (something similar to what we have been experiencing with Brexit currently), concealing the reasons continuing to produce inequities. Multiculturalism was the astute political response to the cultural groups demanding their rights.

Discourses of multiculturalism are often criticised as masquerading discriminatory practices. While in theory multiculturalism protects individuals' diversity, in practice the concept becomes the focal point through which cultural hegemony is created with respect to cultural difference. In Canada, Discourses of multiculturalism support the white-supremacists colonial Discourses (Ng, 2003). For example, research shows that multicultural Discourses normalise Anglophone or Francophone whites as the default Canadian category while other cultural groups are identified as *others* or, in other words, hyphened-Canadians (Bannerji, 2000). According to these perspectives, the application of multiculturalism in daily life creates a fundamental dividing line by which

12 Genealogy of concepts and myths of equity

difference is constructed and otherness is objectified in relation to historically white Anglophone or Francophone Canadians. This is not, however, unusual or unexpected given Canada, as any other nation, is an imagined community and its development to a nation-state is grounded in colonial perspectives.

The implication of this appropriation is that one's identification in this imagined conceptual topography of being Canadian affects the ways in which one makes sense of himself or herself in daily life. In my experience specifically, how I identified myself positioned me in relation to whiteness[7] and defined how I acted when I was a PhD student and a researcher in a university. Such discursive positioning had a direct impact on how I was socialised into normative structures. I was not an outlier or an especially hopeless case. The literature shows that for certain cultural groups, this discursive positioning is a process of alienation; a process through which individuals internalise a false self-system where they accept the oppressor's image of the self (Fanon, 1967). The internalisation of the false self-system works from within, often convincing us that to be normal, to be acceptable, requires degrees of self-negotiation and thus self-alienation (Du Bois, 1994).

Within the online education research, multiculturalism has become a major topic in an attempt to *deal with the problem* of educating an increasingly *diverse* population. Rather than grappling with sociocultural dynamics that may cause unequal social hierarchy, as I have been arguing, the applications of multiculturalism have accepted diversity as inherently beneficial and turned it into a commodity to be marketed. This is evident in the ways in which online education is being promoted. With the increasing number of online programs and exponential growth of students registered in them, the idea of online education has been moving from a small endeavour to a global market that is granting degrees to those who otherwise have no or limited access to higher education. Yet, the idea of multiculturalism grew out of efforts for preserving cultural identity and difference; thus, the debates over multiculturalism are also political debates over identification.

This book, then, aims to provide a more informed and nuanced description of identities and difference in online learning spaces, and how whiteness reproduces inequity when students position themselves in relation to those around them. It explores how macro-level societal Discourses manifest themselves in online learning spaces and operate to produce inequitable learning conditions. It does so by investigating how inequitable learning conditions yield differentiated learning experiences on the basis of participation. The ultimate aim of this book is to rethink the concepts of multiculturalism, diversity, and identities in relation to the teaching and learning practices in online spaces. It does not suggest a blueprint for somehow creating equity. Rather, my aim is to demonstrate why and how inequity might exist in online learning spaces. I aim to create awareness of this perspective for teachers, students, and scholars interested in online education. If we know how and why any such unequal learning conditions occur, we might begin to address them to provide better opportunities

Genealogy of concepts and myths of equity   13

for those who might be disadvantaged. My purpose is exploratory in nature: understanding online learning spaces as the context of learning while social and cultural discourses manifest themselves in ways that people represent themselves and interact with one another. Therefore, this book does not in any way constitute the final word on equity in online spaces; rather, I hope that our understandings of equity in online education will continue to evolve and that this book will serve to spark thought, controversy, debate, and further research.

Finally, I feel it is necessary to define my understanding of equity. I do not regard equity in binary terms – whether something is inequitable or not – nor do I see it as an absolute end. Rather, it is a continuous process and can be understood as the degree to which given conditions are fair for individuals. However, since given conditions can never be equal for individuals in a community, I do not believe any community or group work can ever be inherently equitable. Ultimately, I believe there will always be unjust practices or conditions, whatever the ideological or political system might be. There are, and will be, inevitable inequities in every aspect of civic life. Some of these inequities have been studied, while others have not. This knowledge is as much depressing as it is true and I cannot help but agree with Foucault (1972) that any system of education is a political way of maintaining or modifying the appropriation of discourses, along with the knowledges and powers which they carry.

1.5 Summary

In this chapter, I have demonstrated how social, political, economic, and historical dynamics regarding public schooling and education in general affected the ways in which the theory and practice of online education were developed. I argued that online education literature emerged through and has been hampered by idealistic accounts derived from positivist, modernist, post-Fordist, and liberalist perspectives; perspectives that also shaped the curriculum of public schooling and education. There was and still is an underlying belief that educational use of technology is inherently capable of improving education. The zeitgeist around the time that technology was finding its way into schools and classrooms was that education can be improved by efficiently transmitting academic knowledge to mass amounts of students. Technology was a perfect candidate for this role.

Unfortunately, despite some notable studies (e.g., Cuban, 2001; Selwyn, 2010) the origins and the theoretical assumptions of educational technology and online education are not scrutinised in relation to critical pedagogy. There is a clear need for more accounts and perspectives concerning online education and the social, political, economic, cultural, and historical contexts within which its use (and non-use) is located. Rather than producing yet another recycled account on the limitless potential online education offers, we need more studies questioning the theoretical grounds of online education, not only for recognising its limits but also for working within such limitations. We need

14 Genealogy of concepts and myths of equity

better perspectives, conceptualisations, and frameworks to better understand equity in online spaces. It is only by examining how day-to-day learning practices are historically based on unequal power relations and how such practices operate to reproduce differentiated conditions that we can address questions concerning equity in online education.

Notes

1 (Gee, 2011) uses "big D" Discourses to distinguish it from "little d" discourses; while the first one refers to combination and integration of "language, actions, interactions, ways of thinking, believing, valuing, and using various symbols, tools, and objects to enact a particular sort of socially recognizable identity" (p. 30), the latter one refers to "language-in-use or stretches of language (like conversations or stories)" (p. 34).
2 Such studies focus on the use of audio-visual media and are concerned with transmitting basic knowledge. However, no evidence of actual learning as such are reported since learning was considered as remembering.
3 While efficiency is simply the ratio of input to output, in the case of education, it is defined as the amount of work spent to transmit knowledge. Similarly, in the case of education, productivity is defined as teaching to a mass number of students with little input.
4 Frankfurt School refers to the institute for Social Research at the University of Frankfurt am Main, where interdisciplinary neo-Marxist social theory is developed.
5 Adorno proposed that popular culture can be thought of as a factory producing standardised cultural goods (i.e. films, radio, magazines) that are used to manipulate mass society into passivity. The mechanisation of cultural products is made available by the mass communications media.
6 Habermas was a student in Frankfurt School, and later became the director; however, he is less associated with the Marxist theories. He departed from Marxism and diverged the institute's research agenda.
7 The concept of whiteness denotes sets of norms against which all those who are identified as non-White are judged, measured, and positioned. The concept of whiteness will be discussed in detail later.

References

Adorno, T. W. (2001). *The culture industry: Selected essays on mass culture* (J. M. Bernstein, Ed.). New York, NY: Routledge.

Apple, M. W. (2004). *Ideology and curriculum* (3rd ed.). Boston, MA: Routledge & Kegan Paul.

Aronowitz, S., & Giroux, H. A. (1991). *Postmodern education: Politics, culture, and social criticism.* Minneapolis, MN: University of Minnesota Press.

Bannerji, H. (2000). *Dark side of the nation: Essays on multiculturalism, nationalism and gender.* Toronto, ON: Canadian Scholars' Press.

Bates, T. (2005). *Technology, e-learning and distance education.* New York, NY: Routledge.

Bently, J. P. H., & Tinney, M. V. (2003). *Does culture influence learning? A report on trends in learning styles and preferences across cultures.* Paper presented at the Annual Conference of the Association for Educational Communication & Technology.

Boyd, G. M. (1996). Emancipative educational technology. *Canadian Journal of Educational Communication, 25*(3), 179–186.

Buckingham, D. (2008). Introducing identity. In D. Buckingham (Ed.), *Youth, identity, and digital media* (pp. 1–22). Cambridge, MA: MIT Press Journals.

Clark, R. E. (1983). Reconsidering research on learning from media. *Review of Educational Research, 53*, 445–459. doi:10.3102/00346543053004445

Cuban, L. (2001). *Oversold and underused: Computers in the classroom.* Cambridge, MA: Harvard University Press.

Du Bois, W. E. B. (1994). *The souls of black folk.* New York, NY: Dover Publications.

Ely, D. P. (1999). Toward a philosophy of instructional technology: Thirty years on. *British Journal of Educational Technology, 30*(4), 305–310. doi:10.1111/1467-8535.00120

Esmonde, I. (2009). Mathematics learning in groups: Analyzing equity in two cooperative activity structures. *Journal of the Learning Sciences, 18*(2), 247–284. doi:10.1080/10508400902797958

Evans, T. (1995). Globalisation, post-Fordism and open and distance education. *Distance Education, 16*(2), 256–269. doi:10.1080/0158791950160207

Fanon, F. (1967). *Black skin, white masks* (R. Philcox, Trans., 1st translated ed.). New York, NY: Grove Press.

Feenberg, A. (2002). *Transforming technology: A critical theory revisited* (2nd ed.). New York, NY: Oxford University Press.

Foucault, M. (1972). *The archaeology of knowledge and the discourse on language* (A. M. Sheridan-Smith, Trans.). New York, NY: Pantheon.

Freeman, M., & Bamford, A. (2004). Student choice of anonymity for learner identity in online learning discussion forums. *International Journal on E-Learning, 3*(3), 45–53.

Gee, J. P. (2011). *An introduction to discourse analysis: Theory and method* (3rd ed.). New York, NY: Routledge.

Giroux, H. A. (2011). *On critical pedagogy.* London, UK: Continuum.

Greene, M. (1971). Curriculum and consciousness. *Teachers College Record, 73*(2), 253–270.

Habermas, J. (1984). *The theory of communicative action, Vol. 1: Reason and the rationalization of society* (T. McCarthy, Trans.). Boston, MA: Beacon Press.

Harasim, L. (2000). Shift happens: Online education as a new paradigm in learning. *The Internet and Higher Education, 3*(1–2), 41–61. doi:10.1016/s1096-7516(00)00032-4

Heidegger, M. (1977). *Question concerning technology and other essays* (W. Lovitt, Trans.). New York, NY: Harper Perennial.

Hofstede, G. (1997). *Cultures and organizations: Software of the mind: Intercultural cooperation and its importance for survival.* New York, NY: McGraw-Hill.

Kanuka, H. (2008). Understanding e-learning technologies-in-practice through philosophies-in-practice. In T. Anderson (Ed.), *The theory and practice of online learning* (2nd ed., pp. 75–90). Edmonton, AB: Au Press.

Kim, K.-J., & Bonk, C. J. (2006). Cross-cultural comparisons of online collaboration. *Journal of Computer-Mediated Communication, 8*(1). Retrieved from http://onlinelibrary.wiley.com/doi/10.1111/j.1083-6101.2002.tb00163.x/fulldoi:10.1111/j.1083-6101.2002.tb00163.x

Kliebard, H. M. (1986). *The struggle for the American curriculum, 1893–1958.* New York, NY: Routledge & Kegan Paul.

Ku, H.-Y., Pan, C.-C., Tsai, M.-H., Tao, Y., & Cornell, R. A. (2004). The impact of instructional technology interventions on Asian pedagogy. *Educational Technology Research and Development, 52*(1), 88–92.

McLuhan, M. (1964). *Understanding media: The extensions of man.* New York, NY: McGraw-Hill.

Mills, J., Eyre, G., & Harvey, R. (2005). What makes provision of e-learning successful? Charles Sturt University's experience in Asia. *Education for Information, 23*(1–2), 43–55.

Ng, R. (2003). Toward an integrative approach to equity in education. In P. P. Trifonas (Ed.), *Pedagogies of difference: Rethinking education for social change* (pp. 197–210). New York, NY: Routledge.

Oztok, M., & Brett, C. (2011). Social presence and online learning: A review of research. *The Journal of Distance Education, 25*(3). Retrieved from www.ijede.ca/index.php/jde/article/view/758/1299

Oztok, M., & Kehrwald, B. A. (2017). Social presence reconsidered: Moving beyond, going back, or killing social presence. *Distance Education, 38*(2), 259–266. doi:10.1080/015879 19.2017.1322456

Pinar, W. F. (2004). *What is curriculum theory?* Mahwah, NJ: Lawrence Erlbaum Associates.

Rovai, A. P., & Ponton, M. K. (2005). An examination of sense of classroom community and learning among African American and Caucasian graduate students. *Journal of Asynchronous Learning Networks, 9*(3), 77–92.

Seattler, P. (2004). *The evolution of American educational technology* (2nd Revised ed.). Greenwich, CT: Information Age Publishing.

Selwyn, N. (2010). Looking beyond learning: Notes towards the critical study of educational technology. *Journal of Computer Assisted Learning, 26*(1), 65–73. doi:10.1111/j.1365-2729.2009.00338.x

Sullivan, P. (2001). Gender differences and the online classroom: Male and female college students evaluate their experiences. *Community College Journal of Research and Practice, 25*(10), 805–818. doi:10.1080/106689201753235930

Swan, K., & Shih, L. F. (2005). On the nature and development of social presence in online course discussions. *Journal of Asynchronous Learning Networks, 9*(3), 115–136.

Trend, D. (2001). *Welcome to cyberschool: Education at the crossroads in the information age.* Lanham, MD: Rowman & Littlefield.

Tyler, R. W. (1949). *Basic principles of curriculum and instruction.* Chicago, IL: University of Chicago Press.

Walther, J. B. (1996). Computer-mediated communication: Impersonal, interpersonal, and hyperpersonal interaction. *Communication Research, 23*(1), 3–43. doi:10.1177/0093650 96023001001

Warschauer, M., & Matuchniak, T. (2010). New technology and digital worlds: Analyzing evidence of equity in access, use, and outcomes. *Review of Research in Education, 34*(1), 179–225. doi:10.3102/0091732x09349791

Chapter 2

How to study equity in online spaces

Situating the theoretical frameworks

Equity is a value-laden term and requires human judgement of whether the given circumstances are just or fair. What is just or fair in a given situation, however, is open to philosophical,[1] political,[2] scholarly,[3] or even economic[4] debate. Thus, the definition of equity is contingent upon the contextual judgements of the given situation and may mean different things for different individuals under different circumstances. Indeed, there is no widely agreed-upon understanding of how we might identify it when we see it nor is there a widely agreed-upon way to address it. Nevertheless, the ways in which equity is defined have implications for how equity concerns are addressed.

In this chapter, therefore, I articulate what constitutes equity in online spaces, how I conceptualise equity as situated in pedagogical activities at the micro-level and as being informed by Discourses at the macro-level, and how I examine it in day-to-day online learning practices.

2.1 Equity and Discourses

The first step towards understanding equity in an educational setting is to distinguish it from equality. While equity refers to qualitative judgements of what is right, equality refers to the quantitative measurement of resources, treatment, or outcomes in a given situation. Based on liberal principles, the concept of equality in education calls for meritocracy[5] by offering a theoretical explanation for two issues: maximisation of educational resources and distribution of educational resources. According to this perspective, while the maximisation of resources supports the fundamental liberal values of free choice and neutrality among different ways of life, equalisation of resources supports the use of education to raise the life chances of the least advantaged as far as possible up to those of the most advantaged (Gutmann, 2007). In an educational context, meritocracy argues for distribution of educational resources in proportion to natural ability and willingness to learn.

Research regarding equality in educational settings is concerned with providing sameness in educational treatment, comparing differences found among individuals based on social-demographic characteristics. Thus, many online education studies have addressed quantitative differences or sameness of educational inputs

18 How to study equity in online spaces

or outputs. While the former attends to the equal distribution of resources, such as money spent on school boards or access to digital technologies, the latter focuses on determining the strategies that will result in equal outcomes, such as student dropout rates or test scores.

While equality in educational setting is the first step towards understanding equity in the context of education, it is not a sufficient condition in and of itself. That is, assuming that learning sources, inputs, treatments, or outputs are distributed equally (a dubious supposition, to be sure), we cannot assume learning conditions to be equitable naturally. The context of education is defined by social, political, economic, and historical dynamics; all of which relate to the value-based determination of the resources that set limits while simultaneously enabling particular possibilities across a full range of daily activities. Thus, even if all students are given the same access to the same curricular materials, the same forms of teaching, and the same support for learning, it does not mean that student outcomes will be the same neither does it represent fairness or equity for students' own desires and identities (Gutiérrez, 2007). In other words, conceptualising equity as an outcome of certain treatment cannot help us to decipher how and why inequitable learning conditions might occur. Understanding equity requires a focus both on inequitable social structures and ideologies they give rise to, and on how such realities play out in day-to-day activity in classrooms (Nasir & Cobb, 2007). Thus, the discussion of equity should move beyond investigating whether course-based patterns of various demographic groups are the same; instead, we must consider the pedagogical approaches or practices in which social, political, economic, and historical structures affect day-to-day classroom interactions. We should conceptualise equity as a process that is situated between the tensions of various social structures that exist in any given cultural settings.

Viewing equity as situated in cultural contexts and as involving relations between various social structures requires an examination of how Discourses play a role in the reproduction of social fabric. As a characteristic way of saying, doing, and being, Discourses provide meaning for socially situated identities in socially situated practices (Gee, 2011). According to this perspective, when one presents one's self as a certain kind of person in a certain context, this presentation communicates *a who* and *a what*; while a who is a socially situated identity, a what is a socially situated practice. The subtle yet strong connection between Discourses and the way one makes sense of daily life renders Discourses invisible. Discourses are diffused in the society as individuals reproduce them in their daily lives (Foucault, 1972). The examination of Discourses, then, requires the examination of how socially accepted bodies of thoughts, beliefs, values, and feelings that give meaning to individuals' practices may influence day-to-day practices. In educational research, this means that understanding the role of Discourses require one to investigate how and why individuals feel a need for or are forced to assimilate into mainstream beliefs and values at the expense of their own identities or learning trajectories.

The domination of certain Discourses over individuals – or certain social classes – is referred to as cultural hegemony (Gramsci, 2000). Gramsci uses the concept to explain how ruling elites impose their norms to manipulate and dominate social, cultural, economic, and political beliefs, perceptions, and values in order to reproduce their power and control over the rest of the society. The concept of cultural hegemony provides means to understand how inequity may be reproduced in educational contexts by drawing attention to questions regarding who has control over the conditions for the production of knowledge, values, and classroom practices (Giroux, 2011). In specific, examining cultural hegemony in a given learning space can reveal whose learning is valued as legitimate and how students come to see themselves as members of their learning community. Put differently, the analysis of cultural hegemony can show the ways in which learning spaces can hinder opportunities for individuals to follow their own learning trajectories as Discourses may enforce unfair or unequal conditions for different cultural groups. This means that inequitable learning conditions can occur when individuals identify themselves with the non-dominant perspectives and, as a result, have their values marginalised or their knowledge devalued. If a clear pattern of cultural hegemony is observable over a period of time, forcing students to assimilate into the dominant Discourses, a learning situation can be said to be inequitable.

Discourses, therefore, can link between macro-level social structures in society and the reproduction of inequity at micro-level classroom settings – or online learning spaces. In order to address equity as situated in a pedagogical activity and as being informed by social structures, I employ the concept of Discourses for simultaneously bringing both issues of classroom interaction and broader social, cultural, historical, and political structures to the fore. Fundamental to my perspective is the idea that equity is not about providing a point of sameness among individuals, but about enabling them to become agents of their own learning by appropriating the learning repertoires they need in order to fulfil their potential. Thus, under an equitable learning condition, individuals should be able to build on their prior experiences, construct positive identities as learners without being constrained by the dominant Discourses, and should be accepted as equal partners and treated as such by their peers. Conceptualising equitable pedagogical conditions within the tensions between cultural hegemony and identification, of course, invites a discussion about identification and identities.

2.2 Identity and identification

The concept of identity has been at the centre of many political, philosophical, economic, and academic debates. For example, politically, identity refers to how various social groups struggle for recognition within a society and how these groups are affected by various institutional practices. Philosophically, identity is associated with the question whether humans are unique to

20 How to study equity in online spaces

themselves or they share a degree of sameness with one other in a particular time and space. Academically, it has been deemed vital by many disciplines; yet, identity means different things to different scholars from different disciplines. Indeed, notions of identity are as diverse as the bodies of literature that have taken up the concept. Fields as diverse as psychology, sociology, physical sciences, humanities, and philosophy offer discipline-specific conceptualisations and definitions of identity. Thus, the concept of identity has been overused in academia and its meaning is ambiguous: it may mean too much, too little, or nothing at all (Brubaker & Cooper, 2000).

The concept of identity is challenging: the conundrum becomes evident when the etymology of the word is considered. According to the Oxford English Dictionary, the term was appropriated from a Latin word *idem*, meaning the sameness or being identical. Yet, identity implies both similarity and difference and much of the debate regarding identity stems from the tensions between these two aspects. On the one hand, the concept of identity refers to something unique for each person that is more or less consistent over time; yet on the other hand, it indicates a relationship with a broader social group (Buckingham, 2008). According to this perspective, one's identity is a unique personal biography; that is, who one is varies according to the social context, including others in that particular space as well as personal aims and goals in that particular moment. This dilemma marks the fundamental difference between psychological and sociological perspectives on identity and it remains inherent in educational research.

Psychological perspectives typically contend that individuals have an essential self,[6] assuming that individuals have relatively consistent and stable identities. Identity is seen as internally coherent and inexorable state of being. One's identity, then, is one's struggles over resolving a role confusion. Accordingly, identity is a single state that one achieves over time and development (Erikson, 1968). However, these perspectives do not provide detailed enough means to understand the complex human experience since they do not account for the dynamic interplay of social factors on identity construction (Jenkins, 2008). Psychological perspectives, in this sense, accept identity as a predefined state of self that is independent from or irrelevant to one's experience by ignoring the fluid and contingent nature of identity construction.

Sociological perspectives have moved away from this normative perspective and have suggested that identity is something people enact or perform, as opposed to something people have. According to these perspectives, identities are situated in and bounded by Discourses that exist in any given community. That is, identity is the temporary product of various social factors and it is invoked to highlight the rather unstable, multiple, fluctuating, and fragmented nature of the self (Jenkins, 2008). Precisely because identities are constructed within Discourses, sociological perspectives argue the need for understanding identities as produced through particular practices or enactments in a particular historical, social, and institutional site. Sociological perspectives, therefore,

How to study equity in online spaces   21

move the concept of identity from an understanding of an essential authentic self to a matter of engagement, participation, and membership in a community (Holland, Lachicotte, Jr., Skinner, & Cain, 1998).

In order to better capture and reflect the relationship between Discourses and identity enactments, scholars have employed the concept of identification[7] (or identities-in-practice). Identification draws from the available material and symbolic resources, and it is the process of classifying, labelling, or linking individuals that have a relation to one another (Jenkins, 2008). It is not deterministic in the sense that it is a given, fixed condition, but rather it is situated in contingency and it is socially constructed on the back of a recognition of some shared characteristics with others (Holland et al., 1998). This means that individuals identify themselves or are identified with various cultural categories depending on their enactments of particular identities within particular historical and social situations. In this sense, identification is intrinsic to context. It has both individual and social aspects by which individuals perceive, categorise, and situate themselves, define symbolic boundaries among themselves, create links between one another. When defining their identification, then, people enact their individuality but also to align themselves with others. Questions on how people identify themselves as members of particular groups; how a sense of belonging to that group is developed, sustained, and enhanced requires an approach that appreciates both social and individual levels (Buckingham, 2008). Consequently, identification is a never-ending interplay between Discourses and identity enactments. It is not a singular, fixed, or static entity; rather, it is a dynamic set of practices in particular contexts under particular circumstances (Holland et al., 1998).

Race, gender, and class are the three canonical identity categories by which scholars have investigated identification. As socially constructed identity categories, race, gender, and class are not immaterial or inconsequential; rather, they are informed by and situated in Discourses. The trio of race, gender, and class play a significant role in how different individuals make different meanings of their experiences by affecting how different individuals construct different identifications under particular circumstances. The ways in which they are closely intertwined and the complexity in the ways in which they intersect make it theoretically and practically difficult to talk about them all at once. However, one way to deal with this challenge is to foreground one category while keeping the others, at least analytically, in the background (Gaztambide-Fernández, 2009). This process of analytical shifting between foreground and background provide means to analyse how the dynamics of each category operate distinctly yet in relation to others.

The process of identification, however, needs an interpretative system by which particular meanings or practices can be recognised, legitimised, and prioritised. This interpretative system – or Discourse – provides means for individuals to make sense of themselves by interpreting their moment-by-moment negotiations with others. And, because the process of identification gets its meanings from prevailing Discourses, cultural hegemony can manifest itself by affecting the cultural symbols or signifiers (Holland et al., 1998). That is, while individuals constitute themselves in an active fashion, these practices may not be something freely and openly invented by people themselves. In other words, just because certain identifications are enacted in the moment, it does not mean that people have total freedom to express who they are or act in ways they choose (Foucault, 1972). This concurs with the arguments I provided above that identifications are constructed at the intersection where individuals both act with agency and are acted upon by the social context in which they are positioned. In this sense, identification classifies individuals into readily available subject positions that are derived from the cultural resources at hand. People may resist (especially if they are identified with subaltern categories[8]), redefine, or simply reproduce the identifications available to them.

The relationship between Discourses and the process of identification is important for our understanding of equity. Identifications enable or constrain individuals' access to educational resources or materials. Consciously or unconsciously, individuals may try to identify themselves in line with dominant Discourses in order to gain or secure their access to educational resources or legitimise their learning experiences. Consequently, the process of identification may create inequitable learning conditions. Understanding the macro-level material or symbolic conditions under which identifications are produced at the micro-level educational contexts explains how Discourses can perpetuate inequity since access to the range of meanings available in any given space is determined by how individuals understand themselves and how they are perceived by others. Such an understanding conceptualises both identification and equity as dynamic and practice-based processes in a given cultural context. It underscores the rather implicit yet strong connections between Discourses and inequity in online spaces.

Online education research needs such critical perspectives if it is to adequately address equity and social justice in learning contexts. Critical questions should revolve around how claims of identification are produced in a particular situation and how those claims affect individuals' experiences. Research should explore how identifications play a role in access to or distribution of learning resources, rather than simply investigating how a particular person or group experiences online learning. It is through examining how Discourses manifest themselves in the process of identification that we can work within analytical frameworks and actively make contextual judgements of equity.

2.3 Online selves and impression management

In other disciplines, such as Information and Communication Studies, Cultural Studies, or Computer Sciences, research regarding the intersections of technology, mediated interactions, and identification has a relatively long history. For example, early research examined how interactions within and through online spaces allow individuals to manage identifications (e.g., Giese, 1998; Hardey, 2002; Walker, 2000). Later, scholars started pay more attention to the subjective side of technology. Research has questioned what technology does to us and discussed how a mediated experience results in new manifestations of identity. The current perspectives build on these early accounts and indicate that face-to-face embodied experiences are reproduced in online spaces (Walther, 2007). Accordingly, one way to conceptualise identification in online spaces should be to focus on how individuals manage their online selves.

Online selves are created through profile pages and they are situated within the intersection of self-representation and identification. Yet, what is taken for granted in face-to-face contexts cannot be taken for granted in online spaces. While physical presence conveys cues about one's gender, race, social-status, age group, attitudes, or affiliations, etc. by its very being, online self has to be created. In order to convey social cues, individuals use everyday realities when they write digital bodies (Sundén, 2003). Online self is tightly bound by the individual behind the profile because it is a direct digital representation of that person in online spaces. Thus, the performances, enactments, presentations that take place in online spaces are not isolated acts neither are they disconnected from face-to-face settings; rather, these are conscious actions that rely on a context that spans on both face-to-face and online spaces (boyd, 2008). A digital body, similar to a body in face-to-face settings, not only identifies a person in relation to those around them but also situates a person in a social context. Thus, the pressure surrounding creating a profile page is not much different than representing the self in daily life. Online self is contextual and ephemeral. Research reported on Walker (2000)'s work shows that identity statements on profile pages closely resemble those found in face-to-face interaction. According to this study, profile pages can give and give off impressions: they can be compared to old-fashioned physical objects; they can invite response and create dialogue. It is important to note that writing up a digital-self is not, by any means, limited to creating profile pages. People are able to represent themselves – at least to a certain extent – even if profile pages are not present. In the absence of profile pages, one uses linguistic signs and markers as semiotic resources since such linguistic-semiotic signs bear sociocultural knowledge and provide contextualising cues.

Creation of online selves – whether in an online learning space, Facebook, Twitter, Instagram, or any other social media platform – resemble the process of identification in face-to-face contexts: people type in how they wish to represent themselves and include information about their sense of self in relation to those around them. Regardless of the type of the online space or the combination of media used, people explicitly articulate their identity, imagine the context in which they are operating, and negotiate the impressions they are conveying (boyd, 2008). Creating an online self, however, is the beginning of the process of identification in online spaces. The presentation of self in everyday life is more than simply introducing oneself but a *theatrical performance* balanced between the dynamics of what one expressed and how one impressed. In order to make a good impression, people look around, observe how others are behaving, and enact their performances accordingly. This is what Goffman (1959) calls impression management to explain how people alter their behaviour in order to be perceived as intended.

While Goffman developed his notion in face-to-face contexts, impression management in online spaces is no exception. Tightly connected to the context in which impression management takes place, people manage their impressions in online spaces – and mostly create better selves. The notion of better selves is based on the comparison between online self and face-to-face self with respect to the physical appearance. For Turkle (2011), people tend to represent themselves as more desirable and better looking: online selves are usually thinner, slimmer, or more athletic. While this is based on a normative understanding of beauty, the idea of better self is tightly connected to the context and there can be many ways in which better selves can be constructed. In online education, better self has an impact on how students present themselves as smart, reliable, and hard-working individuals – which will be discussed later.

All these accounts and perspectives indicate that despite the absence of physical bodies, people create a digital body – an online self, through which people embody material and symbolic conditions of daily life in online contexts. Online space, in this sense, is shaped by and grounded in the social, political, economic, and historical realities of its inhabitants; it is not a *tabula rasa*.

2.4 Social presence and social absence

While early research studied online and offline practices as isolated entities, later accounts have challenged such perspectives and argued that online and offline beings should not be studied as a dichotomy. In fact, when the waning differences between real and virtual are coupled with the ubiquitous of nature of social media, it is possible to argue that there is no such notion as offline (Turkle, 2011). They are continuous states of the same being.

The concept of presence[9] has been employed to study being in online space. Defined as the degree to which individuals represent themselves and perceive others in online spaces, social presence has long been employed to study human experience in online learning spaces (Oztok & Brett, 2011). Social presence is deemed as the total quality of interpersonal relationships (Kehrwald, 2010) allowing individuals to engage with each other by interacting with and reacting to others (Hill, Song, & West, 2009). The construction of social presence is grounded in how individuals enact their identification – or perform their online self as they socialise in an online space. Social presence, in this sense, is constructed dialogically and it is a combination of the self and others: it operates on the boundary between two consciousnesses, two subjects. As a dialogic construction, it conveys meanings about individuals and mediates sociocultural norms, values, beliefs, and perspectives that individuals bring into online learning spaces. Consequently, the construction of social presence is not an improvisation without a script but is derived from cultural norms and thus is constrained by Discourses (Walther, 2007). By accepting, rejecting, redefining, or simply reproducing their subjectivities in their social presence, individuals enact their ways of being in online learning spaces.

Understanding the relation of the concept of social presence to cultural hegemony (and thus to equity) goes beyond how individuals simply represent themselves depending on their perceptions of self in relation to others and further includes a discussion on the qualities and cultural background that individuals consciously filter out when they create their online existence. That is, the process of identification in online experiences is not only articulated by what is represented but also defined by what is filtered out in that particular representation. I shall term these consciously filtered-out identifications 'social absence'. Therefore, I regard social absence as the extent to which particular identifications are not represented in one's online being. Social absence is not the opposite of social presence; rather, presence and absence work together to define one's online self. Social presence and social absence are always related to each other and both are situated in and defined by Discourses.

In online spaces, one's social presence or social absence operate as a site for the process of identification, a process of conveying who they are to other people. In specific, individuals assess the context in which they enact their identification and consider the conditions by which others will make sense of their online self. Then, individuals adjust their level of social presence and social absence in particular ways in order to be accepted or legitimised. This process of interpretation, adjustment, and enactment of self-representation is the same exact process that Goffman (1959) called impression management. It is through the process of impression management that individuals write themselves into online beings (boyd, 2008). Online self, then, can be accepted as a continuous process of decision making about social presence and social absence.

Being able to read social context and react accordingly is fundamental to being socialised into a society. However, this socialisation process does not operate in uniformity across different cohorts of students. Socialisation in online spaces can be thought of as the process by which people from certain cultural groups can hide their differences since the difference is the primary point of othering,[10] constituting a fixated form of representation for both the dominant and the subaltern (Spivak, 1999). Social absence, therefore, can provide means to explore the degree to which individuals hide their differences in online spaces as they socialise into their communities. Consequently, one's social presence or absence is contingent on the dynamics of what constitutes the subaltern or how the others are defined.

It is important to distinguish social absence from the notion of anonymity. According to the Oxford Online Dictionary, anonymity is used to describe situations where the person in question is non-identifiable, unreachable, or untraceable; it refers to an unknown person. As a constituting element of online identification, the concept of social absence is different as it helps with understanding the online self while anonymity increases the level of impersonality. However, despite such disparities, the concept of social absence can provide theoretical lenses to explain why individuals hide behind their relative anonymity to overcome exclusion based on their sociocultural identifications (Rogers & Lea, 2005). For example, the research described in Gunawardena and Zittle's (1997) study reports that when individuals had lower levels of social presence (this should be read as: thus higher levels of social absence), they perceived that the impersonal nature of online engagements provided them more equal opportunities to participate. Unfortunately, that study does not further explain the correlation between low levels of social presence and sense of impersonality, neither does it extend the analysis to explain why participants felt online space to be impersonal. Similarly, research reported in Ferreday, Hodgson, and Jones's (2006) work indicates that although the participants did not generally perceive gender as an issue in their everyday interactions, a female student articulated that gender differences did not completely disappear. The female student in that study characterised her experience as an ideal blend of personalities as she was performing a stereotypical masculinity[11] by being more macho since she was situated in a male-dominated space. In this example, her social absence (the extent that she filtered out her femininity but performed masculinity) can typify how individuals try to be identified with dominant identifications in order to avoid exclusion.

In order to understand what these dominant identifications mean and how they are constructed, I examine the context in which and cultural practices by which social presence and absence are created: the community. Educational research has long studied the concept of community.[12] Defined as a group of individuals who collaboratively engage in purposeful dialogue to construct personal meaning and confirm mutual understandings, the concept of community has been employed to explain what the online learning context is, how it plays a role in learning, how it relates to online culture, and how it mediates pedagogy (Rheingold, 2000). The central idea of the community is that it is built around the mutuality of meanings, purposes, and practices and that culture mediates these meanings, purposes, and practices. Mutuality of meanings and goals, surely, are very important for learning practices. However, mutual meanings may not always support a sense of community but can have consequences for particular individuals or groups; particularly when being a member of a community requires individuals to accept (or seem to accept) its core values and norms in order to preserve the integrity of the community. By accepting or rejecting their communities' mutual meanings, individuals can be included into or excluded from their communities. Thus, in order to be included as a member of a community and be legitimised in their participation, individuals may feel pressured to accept such mutual meanings.

The process of developing a sense of belonging to a community is closely related to how individuals make sense of themselves and others; in other words,

How to study equity in online spaces   27

it is closely related to social presence and social absence. Nevertheless, a community is not a zero-institution.[13] Any given space is a direct embodiment of Discourses in its purest manifestation and the struggle for how this space be overdetermined is precisely the struggle for cultural hegemony (Zizek, 2008). It is through this battle for hegemony that the online learning space can create conditions for inequitable learning situations. Consensus or group cohesion plays a large role in online discussions and it is fairly common for members to silence, modify, or limit the dissenting voices in favour of the dominant opinion (Oztok, 2016). How mutual meanings are negotiated and defined, therefore, plays a role in how individuals perceive themselves and thus impacts how they construct their social presence and absence.

Every educational system, including online education, reproduces social disputes and struggles; thus, it is a political means of maintaining or modifying the Discourses – with the knowledge and the powers they carry with them (Foucault, 1972). Consequently, ignoring the questions concerning whose values, perspectives, and beliefs are legitimised as mutual meanings can lead to inequitable learning situations since such mutual meanings can reproduce cultural hegemony by compelling individuals to filter out their particular subjectivities in order to be identified with dominant Discourses.

2.5 Researching individuals in online learning

This ethnographic work is interested in understanding how inequity is reproduced in online learning spaces when macro-level social Discourses come into play and affect individuals' micro-level learning experiences. Even though the literature on equity is slowly growing, there remains a lack of clear understanding for addressing and investigating inequitable learning experiences in relation to Discourses. However, scholars suggest that equity-oriented research should probe how students experience their learning activities (Esmonde, 2009). Thus, I am concerned with exploring how students' experiences are situated within and related to Discourses of identification. Specifically, I analyse how whiteness as a Discourse of identification enables or constrains students' social engagements with one another and negotiations of meanings. In conjunction with Discourses of identification, I further probe how students negotiate the norms of participation in their daily online learning practices.

Yet, understanding the online experience is an epistemologically and methodologically challenging task for researchers since the Internet as a research context aggravates the challenges of doing good enough qualitative research (Baym, 2009). Although very old – and perhaps not even funny anymore – the cartoon published by the *New Yorker* magazine in 1993 can be one example to explain the epistemological problems associated with doing online research. The cartoon features two dogs, one sitting on a chair in front of a computer, speaking to a second dog sitting on the floor: "On the Internet, nobody knows you are a dog". There are many ways to interpret the message of this cartoon.

For example, while it may refer to the relative anonymity of individuals on the Internet, it may mean that one can bend his or her identity, pretending to be someone else. In general, the cartoon symbolises the understanding that identification and online experience – or even dogness – needs to be contextualised. In what follows, I shall articulate, discuss, and justify my contextualisation.

Researchers continuously make decisions about what is to be gained or lost with each option that lies before them. These decisions have never been about distinguishing right from wrong in an absolute manner but about finding the most appropriate ways of collecting, interpreting, and presenting data within the given circumstances. Thus, my decisions were always open-ended and subject to constant reinterpretation, determined by my goal of capturing and reflecting the online experiences. Below, I outline the conceptual, epistemological, and methodological decisions that I made. While some of the decisions I made are specific for the online context, many of the struggles I encountered are germane to all types of qualitative research. I do not suggest my methodological decisions to be accepted as one absolute explanation; rather, I do hope that I provide an alternative way to think about an ongoing discussion about doing Internet research.

2.5.1 The Internet as a research site: understanding and defining the research site

Studying equity and social justice in online education is thrilling. Yet, studying online space as a research context is ontologically, epistemologically, theoretically, and methodologically challenging. What constitutes the context for online education? What does it mean for an individual to experience the online context? How can I know about, study, explore, and articulate one's online experiences? Another relevant concern regarding the research site is whether the site is discovered or constructed; and if it is constructed, whether it is constructed by the participants or by the researcher. Current perspectives, particularly informed by Marxist, feminist, or post-colonial traditions, suggest that the research site is constructed both by participants and by the researcher.

This perspective makes evident the importance of researcher-participant interaction in understanding the phenomenon under study. Furthermore, the co-construction of the research site not only defines the ways in which the researcher comes to understand the phenomenon, but also determines how he or she defines and supports the validity of the constructed reality. I accept validity in its traditional sense; that is, I refer to the accuracy and truthfulness of research in the attempt to define and describe the reality. Surely, the accuracy and truthfulness of the reality are tightly related to one's epistemological and methodological perspectives. My perspective is an integrative approach: conducting an empirical inquiry into social reality, which takes into account that the reality is in fact a mosaic of different realities and that my inquiry is part of the processes forming this social mosaic (Saukko, 2005).

2.5.1.1 Epistemological puzzles

Conceptualising online spaces has always been at the centre of scholarly debates. Early scholarship concerning experiences in online spaces offered science-fictionalised perspectives, arguing that the Internet is a culture by itself, where social, political, and historical realities of daily life are left behind (for example, see, Barlow, 1996; Stone, 1995). As researchers began focusing on how individuals appropriate the Internet and incorporate it into their lives, they moved from this rhetoric to show that material and symbolic realities of daily life play crucial roles in individuals' online experiences. For instance, the Internet researchers articulated that social constructions are reproduced online and that one's socio-historical context is an integral part of how one makes sense of their online selves (Turkle, 2011). Current perspectives moved from the cyber-utopian understanding and conceptualise online spaces as the natural part of daily life (Ito, 2010). According to these perspectives, the Internet exists within the broader cultural context in which people live; yet, it possesses a set of norms and practices that are unique to itself. That is, online experiences extend the physical while also being configured by the digital (Sundén, 2003).

In order to understand the online experience, therefore, I focus on the ways in which individuals co-construct the material and symbolic realities of the daily life in online spaces. I look for the interconnections and interplays between the online learning space and the context within which it is situated. In specific, I trace the flows of individuals, utilisation of Discourses, and cultivation of meanings in online spaces.

2.5.1.2 Methodological puzzles

On the theoretical and methodological level, I struggled to decide on a research site that is balanced between the tension of the breadth and depth of the research site. What constitutes the research site for online education? How can I define the boundaries of the research field in a theoretically boundless web space? I made a decision through a painful process of self-debates about how I can capture and represent issues of social justice and equity. I decided to focus on online courses offered at universities since the literature of online education greatly focuses on online education in higher education institutions. Yet, online courses offered at universities cannot be accepted as one unified research site; online courses can be classified in virtually limitless ways. For example, the method of delivery (i.e. fully online or blended), subject matter (i.e. group discussions or individual virtual lab sessions), academic level (i.e. graduate courses or undergraduate courses), or access method (i.e. synchronous or asynchronous) can significantly alter how one experiences online learning.

For the accounts reported in this book, I did not used predefined criteria for deciding the research site but let the phenomenon itself determine the selection of online courses. Theoretically and methodologically, three conditions

30 How to study equity in online spaces

emerged for deciding on a good enough research site investigating social justice and equity in online education. First, the online course should have an optimum class size to provide optimum engagement among students due to a critical mass to support online discussions (Hewitt & Brett, 2007). Second, the online course should be based on asynchronous discussions, where individuals are required to interact and engage with each other. Third, the online course should encourage and support social ties and bonds in order for individuals to feel the sense of community.

2.5.2 Entering the research site: the online self as the online researcher

There are many epistemological quandaries to address when deciding on what constitutes the research site and what defining its boundaries requires. Yet, such decisions do not provide any practical solution for entering the research field neither do they ease negotiating my insider/outsider status. Entering the research site is a complex process of negotiations due to the dynamic relationship between the researcher and the participants. In all of my engagements with my participants, whether online or face-to-face, I was conscious of my own identification in relation to who, what, and where I was studying. I gained access to the online learning space a week before the official start day and created my profile page – my online self, making my presence known and explicit to others. Furthermore, in order to make my presence as explicit as it could be, I shared a YouTube video in the social area of this learning space, in which I introduced myself and my research, and invited students to participate in my research.

While my profile page and the YouTube video introduced me and my research, my interactions with participants were subject to constant tensions. This was particularly true for the dynamics related to my status of being insider and outsider; the status that is particularly important for any ethnographer to understand the perspectives of the people being studied. I believe that either status is not entirely possible nor is it a static dichotomy; rather, being an insider or outsider is a dynamic process that is negotiated when an ethnographer engages with the participants. Thus, if the essence of ethnographic work is to develop a perspective that accounts for both understanding people's perspectives from the inside while also viewing them distantly (Hammersley, 2006), my online self as a researcher was pivotal for me to develop this perspective.

There were many aspects through which I switched between my insider and outsider status. Studying equity and social justice in online education with respect to race and ethnicity inevitably created a tension around my ethnic and racial background. As I have already discussed in Chapter 1, my identification as "not white enough" enabled me to be an insider for those who are identified as non-white while at the same time an outsider for those who are identified as white. In one of my interviews with one white participant, I put my arm next to her arm and we compared our skin colour. She was surprised to see that my skin tone was paler, and she admitted that I can pretend to be white if I do not speak English (because of my particular accent). Collecting data from graduate-level online courses provided another aspect by which I was able to exploit my insider and outsider status. I was not a faculty member but just a researcher, whom they can easily talk to since I was literally on the same hierarchical level with my participants. Indeed, in many cases, we kept talking for many hours after I officially ended the interview protocol and stopped the voice recorder. My experience with online courses gave me one more aspect by which I identified myself as insider. I took many online courses (in fact, I took the very same courses earlier in which I collected my data) and I was very familiar with the troubles that participants were going through.

2.5.3 The online data: techniques, methods, sources, avenues

In this ethnographic work, I used a combination of techniques, including in-depth interviews, participant observation, a student questionnaire, and discourse analysis. The bulk of data used in my analysis stems from in-depth interviews; yet, each data set in combination reveals particular and overlapping areas of the phenomenon under study. This triangulation method informs and influences the interpretation of the other data forms. What follows is a description of the different types of data that were obtained and used as part of my field research.

I conducted three in-depth interviews at the beginning, in the middle, and at the end of the study. All interview protocols included open-ended and semi-structured questions, focusing on different aspects of participants' online learning experience. At the end of the second and the third interviews, I shared my initial thoughts with interviewees and asked them to clarify or challenge my thoughts in order to seek contradictory evidence for my own understanding. By doing this, I specifically aimed to avoid defining the reality from the outside but invited participants to do analysis with me for explaining the reality from both the inside and outside. Taken together, in-depth interviews provided a collection of data about how individuals make sense of themselves, of their peers, and of their experiences in online learning contexts.

Participant observation is a canonical tool for any ethnographic work. Many researchers conduct their participant observation as they *deeply hang out* in the context, a term coined by Geertz (1973) to describe the process of immersing in a cultural experience. My participant observation constitutes my direct engagements with participants, along with the quantitative tracking data that is automatically generated by the computer to analyse what students do in the online learning space. Despite spending about 300 hours online, I do not refer to my participant observation as "deep hanging out". Rather, I refer to my participant observation as getting to know my participants. I used my observation data to get a general sense of what students do when they log in to the online space. My aim with the participant observation was to identify patterns and norms of engagements among individuals, which I discussed with my participants later in interviews.

At the beginning of this work, I administered an online questionnaire with open-ended and free-response questions, allowing participants to describe themselves in their own words. The questionnaire generated data about the demographics of participants and their daily professional and personal life outside the online learning space, providing me preliminary data about participants before I conducted interviews.

Discourse analysis – discourse as language-in-use – is a technique employed to explore how language mediates between meanings, practices, and social structures. It reveals how language regulates particular forms of meanings, identities, and social experiences by deconstructing the relationships among saying, doing, and being. There were three avenues for discourse analysis: asynchronous weekly discussions, learning journals,[14] and online selves.

Online asynchronous discussions are not simply a means for arriving at decisions but convey implicit or explicit meanings. They are social, historical, and political artefacts. The discourse analysis of asynchronous discussions provided rich data for exploring how Discourses of identification manifest themselves and affect negotiations of meanings. Learning journals allowed students to articulate their learning experiences as they reflect on what they have learned about the subject matter and how they have learned it in that particular week. The discourse analysis, therefore, revealed how Discourses of identification manifested in how individuals made sense of themselves as students, of their peers, and of the subject matter. These entries provided additional information about individuals' perspectives. I used this data to counter or complement the broader data that I gathered. Online selves, as I have argued above, is a process by which students represent themselves and create their existence online. Deconstructing online selves offered rich data to analyse whiteness as a Discourse of identification and enabled me to investigate the otherwise hidden effects of Discourses on individuals' learning experiences. I used data from online selves during my interviews with my participants, aiming to make sense of how they thought about their identification.

Notes

1 Philosophy of ethics (or values) is concerned with systematising, defending, and recommending concepts of right and wrong behaviour. Philosophical debate focuses on how we understand, know about, and what we mean when we talk about what is right and what is wrong.
2 Ethical politics is the political terrain in which the right way to live is subject to contest, but there is not necessarily any contest for state power or any attempt to seek office or build organisations.
3 Scholars have tried to explain how, why, and to what degree people value things; whether the thing is a person, idea, object, or anything else. Scholarly debates revolve around

the idea that different groups of people may hold or prioritise different kinds of values influencing social behaviour.

4 Economic debate emphasises the consumer's choices as evidence that a particular thing is of value.

5 Meritocracy argues that resources, rights, and responsibilities should be objectively assigned to individuals based upon their merits (i.e. intelligence, credentials, and education) determined through evaluations or examinations. In education, merits are conceptualised in terms of competency and ability, measured by standardised achievement tests. In its most neo-liberal interpretation, meritocracy is associated with the concept of Social-Darwinism, suggesting that the resources must be given to those who deserve them.

6 Post-structuralist argument criticises essentialism by focusing on the oppressive and reductive function of representation and argues that the idea of "essential self" risks naturalising one group's experience as normative; thereby, it marginalises other groups and creates exclusion.

7 While sociologists reacted to essentialist psychological perspectives, ironically enough, the concept itself is historically associated with Freud and his method of psychoanalysis. Jacques Lacan, another psychoanalyst, has also made prominent contributions to the psychological aspects of the term by developing Freud's concepts.

8 While the term is derived from Gramsci's work, it is associated with post-colonial theorists, particularly with Edward Said and Gayatri Spivak. It describes the social groups who are socially, politically, and geographically outside of the hegemonic power structures, thus, those who are excluded from a society's established structures for political representation.

9 While online education scholars have adopted the term in the 1980s to study the various experiences in online learning spaces, presence research originated in the discipline of Communication Studies and, indeed, the term is coined by scholars in this discipline (see Short, Williams, & Christie, 1976). Communication Studies research has long examined the effects of technology on the representation of mind and body. See Floridi (2005) for a detailed discussion.

10 The other is a stereotypical form of identification and fixed mode of representation. Othering is a process by which societies form and sustain symbolic boundaries through cultural hegemony in order to exclude or segregate whom they want to subordinate. By marginalising subordinate cultures' perspectives or extenuating their experiences, the dominant culture articulates its difference and reproduces cultural hegemony.

11 It is important to note that I do not define what male behaviours might be nor do I suggest what it means to be a male or female; neither do I argue that masculinity can only be associated with males.

12 Some scholars termed special communities based on the context or the purposes, such as Community of Inquiry (Garrison, Anderson, & Archer, 1999), Knowledge Building Communities (Scardamalia & Bereiter, 1994), Virtual Communities (Hiltz, 1994), or Communities of Practice (Wenger, 1998). I do not specifically refer to any of these definitions but use the community in its most general definition.

13 Lévi-Strauss (1967) uses the term to define a hypothetical institution with no determinate function since relationships within this social group are natural and have no predetermined meanings.

14 This is a rather unusual pedagogical practice for many online education scholars and instructors. Technically, it is a forum within the online learning environment, where students can post blog-like entries and reflect their insights. Learning journals are described by the instructor of these online courses in the following way:

> your entries will involve a process of emergent understanding and ideas which may shift a lot between early and later in the course, and that is fine. These entries

34 How to study equity in online spaces

are a way to connect with others interested in similar ideas, and to think about ideas you come across online and in other contexts, in relation to your own academic development and identity.

References

Barlow, J. P. (1996). A declaration of the independence of cyberspace. *Electronic Frontier Foundation*. Retrieved from https://www.eff.org/cyberspace-independence

Baym, N. (2009). What constitutes quality in qualitative internet research? In A. Markham & N. Baym (Eds.), *Internet inquiry: Conversations about method* (pp. 173–189). Thousands Oak, CA: Sage Publications.

boyd, d. (2008). Why youth ♥ social network sites: The role of networked publics in teenage social life. In D. Buckingham (Ed.), *Youth, identity, and digital media* (pp. 119–142). Cambridge, MA: MIT Press Journals.

Brubaker, R., & Cooper, F. (2000). Beyond "identity". *Theory and Society, 29*(1), 1–47. doi:10.1023/a:1007068714468

Buckingham, D. (2008). Introducing identity. In D. Buckingham (Ed.), *Youth, identity, and digital media* (pp. 1–22). Cambridge, MA: MIT Press Journals.

Erikson, E. H. (1968). *Identity: Youth and crisis*. New York, NY: Norton.

Esmonde, I. (2009). Ideas and identities: Supporting equity in cooperative mathematics learning. *Review of Educational Research, 79*(2), 1008–1043. doi:10.3102/0034654309332562

Ferreday, D., Hodgson, V., & Jones, C. (2006). Dialogue, language and identity: Critical issues for networked management learning. *Studies in Continuing Education, 28*(3), 223–239. doi:10.1080/01580370600947389

Floridi, L. (2005). The philosophy of presence: From epistemic failure to successful observation. *Presence: Teleoperators and Virtual Environments, 14*(6), 656–667. doi:10.1162/105474605775196553

Foucault, M. (1972). *The archaeology of knowledge and the discourse on language* (A. M. Sheridan-Smith, Trans.). New York, NY: Pantheon.

Garrison, D. R., Anderson, T., & Archer, W. (1999). Critical inquiry in a text-based environment: Computer conferencing in higher education. *The Internet and Higher Education, 2*(2–3), 87–105. doi:10.1016/s1096-7516(00)00016-6

Gaztambide-Fernández, R. (2009). *The best of the best: Becoming elite at an American boarding school*. Cambridge, MA: Harvard University Press.

Gee, J. P. (2011). *An introduction to discourse analysis: Theory and method* (3rd ed.). New York, NY: Routledge.

Geertz, C. (1973). *The interpretation of cultures*. New York, NY: Basic Books.

Giese, M. (1998). Self without body: Textual self-representation in an electronic community. *First Monday, 3*(4). Retrieved from http://pear.accc.uic.edu/ojs/index.php/fm/article/view/587/508doi:10.5210/fm.v3i4.587

Giroux, H. A. (2011). *On critical pedagogy*. London, UK: Continuum.

Goffman, E. (1959). *The presentation of self in everyday life*. New York, NY: Anchor Books.

Gramsci, A. (2000). *An Antonio Gramsci reader: Selected writings 1916–1935* (D. Forgacs, Ed.). New York, NY: Schocken Books.

Gunawardena, C. N., & Zittle, F. J. (1997). Social presence as a predictor of satisfaction within a computer-mediated conferencing environment. *American Journal of Distance Education, 11*(3), 8–26. doi:10.1080/08923649709526970

How to study equity in online spaces 35

Gutiérrez, R. (2007). (Re)defining equity: The importance of a critical perspective. In N. I. S. Nasir & P. Cobb (Eds.), *Improving access to mathematics: Diversity and equity in the classroom* (pp. 37–50). New York, NY: Teachers College Press.

Gutmann, A. (2007). Interpreting equal educational opportunity. In R. Curren (Ed.), *Philosophy of education: An anthology* (pp. 236–242). Malden, MA: Blackwell.

Hammersley, M. (2006). Ethnography: Problems and prospects. *Ethnography and Education*, *1*(1), 3–14. doi:10.1080/17457820500512697

Hardey, M. (2002). Life beyond the screen: Embodiment and identity through the internet. *The Sociological Review*, *50*(4), 570–585. doi:10.1111/1467-954x.00399

Hewitt, J., & Brett, C. (2007). The relationship between class size and online activity patterns in asynchronous computer conferencing environments. *Computers & Education*, *49*(4), 1258–1271. doi:10.1016/j.compedu.2006.02.001

Hill, J. R., Song, L., & West, R. E. (2009). Social learning theory and web-based learning environments: A review of research and discussion of implications. *American Journal of Distance Education*, *23*(2), 88–103. doi:10.1080/08923640902857713

Hiltz, S. R. (1994). *The virtual classroom: Learning without limits via computer networks*. Norwood, NJ: Ablex.

Holland, D., Lachicotte, Jr., W., Skinner, D., & Cain, C. (1998). *Identity and agency in cultural worlds*. Cambridge, MA: Harvard University Press.

Ito, M. (2010). *Hanging out, messing around, and geeking out: Kids living and learning with new media*. Cambridge, MA: MIT Press.

Jenkins, R. (2008). *Social identity* (3rd ed.). New York, NY: Taylor & Francis.

Kehrwald, B. (2010). Being online: Social presence as subjectivity in online learning. *London Review of Education*, *8*(1), 39–50. doi:10.1080/14748460903557688

Lévi-Strauss, C. (1967). *Structural anthropology* (C. Jacobson & B. G. Schoepf, Trans.). New York, NY: Anchor Books.

Nasir, N. I. S., & Cobb, P. (2007). Introduction. In N. I. S. Nasir & P. Cobb (Eds.), *Improving access to mathematics: Diversity and equity in the classroom* (pp. 1–9). New York, NY: Teachers College Press.

Oztok, M. (2016). Cultural ways of constructing knowledge: The role of identities in online group discussions. *International Journal of Computer-Supported Collaborative Learning*, *11*(2), 157–186. doi:10.1007/s11412-016-9233-7

Oztok, M., & Brett, C. (2011). Social presence and online learning: A review of research. *The Journal of Distance Education*, *25*(3). Retrieved from www.ijede.ca/index.php/jde/article/view/758/1299

Rheingold, H. (2000). *The virtual community: Homesteading on the electronic frontier*. Cambridge, MA: MIT Press.

Rogers, P., & Lea, M. (2005). Social presence in distributed group environments: The role of social identity. *Behaviour & Information Technology*, *24*(2), 151–158. doi:10.1080/0144 9290410001723472

Saukko, P. (2005). Methodologies for cultural studies: An integrative approach. In N. K. Denzin & Y. S. Lincoln (Eds.), *The Sage handbook of qualitative research* (3rd ed., pp. 343–356). Thousands Oak, CA: Sage Publications.

Scardamalia, M., & Bereiter, C. (1994). Computer support for knowledge-building communities. *Journal of the Learning Sciences*, *3*(3), 265–283. doi:10.1207/s15327809jls0303_3

Short, J., Williams, E., & Christie, B. (1976). *The social psychology of telecommunications*. London, UK: Wiley.

Spivak, G. C. (1999). *A critique of postcolonial reason: Toward a history of the vanishing present.* Cambridge, MA: Harvard University Press.

Stone, A. R. (1995). *The war of desire and technology at the close of the mechanical age.* Cambridge, MA: MIT Press.

Sundén, J. (2003). *Material virtualities: Approaching online textual embodiment.* New York, NY: Peter Lang Publishing.

Turkle, S. (2011). *Alone together: Why we expect more from technology and less from each other.* New York, NY: Basic Books.

Walker, K. (2000). "It's difficult to hide it": The presentation of self on internet home pages. *Qualitative Sociology, 23*(1), 99–120. doi:10.1023/a:1005407717409

Walther, J. B. (2007). Selective self-presentation in computer-mediated communication: Hyperpersonal dimensions of technology, language, and cognition. *Computers in Human Behavior, 23*(5), 2538–2557. doi:10.1016/j.chb.2006.05.002

Wenger, E. (1998). *Communities of practice: Learning, meaning, and identity.* Cambridge, UK: Cambridge University Press.

Zizek, S. (2008). *The plague of fantasies.* New York, NY: Verso.

Chapter 3

Writing oneself into online being

The art of self-representation and impression management

Online selves convey social cues about an individual through which one can be positioned within a social context. As I explained in Chapter 2, identification is a dynamic process that is defined and shaped by socio-historical variables at hand. In this chapter, therefore, I illustrate how online selves are created through a dynamic process of identification and how, in return, online selves operationalise impression management.

Creating an online self and crafting it has both technological and sociocultural aspects. Technologically, it is an easy task even for novice users; it requires one to create an online account (in this case, an account in the online space) and follow screen prompts throughout predefined procedures. Consider, for example, this passage from my field notes about the technical aspects of creating my online self for this research:

> I type the online course's address in my web browser's address bar and hit the return key. A page is loaded with an image in the background showing one of the many historical landmark buildings of the university, asking for my user name and password. I successfully enter my name and password and sign in to the online space. The browser takes me directly to the "community" area (are we a community already?), though I am the only one in the space at the moment (the course allows you to see who else is online and there is no option to hide out). I feel like a student who arrives to the lecture hall earlier than anyone else and sits there alone waiting for other students to come in though I am very much aware that people might log in and out of the space anytime due to the asynchronous nature of the space. I play around with the buttons that I can click and check the menus to figure out what my options are. I realise that the banner on top of the web page is the picture of the school's building and it is indicating the code and name of the course, creating a sense of reality and belongingness as though it is a real classroom. It all makes sense to me.

With nobody around to talk to, I click on my avatar – a little picture representing me – and take a close look at my online self, my online representation:

> I am a beautiful purplish and whitish daisy (a random picture that is assigned to my online account by the system). I go into the preferences

menu, where I can edit my account settings and change my picture. I enter some information regarding my time zone and location. I change my profile picture to a picture of myself that I uploaded to the system though I am wondering whether I should keep the daisy since it is better to look at a flower than to look at myself. I decide to go with my own picture anyway since I know representing myself as who I am is an important dynamic in the delicate balance of intimacy between me and my participants. I want them to know me as much as I can represent myself to them.

While changing basic information and uploading a picture is a technologically simple process, how to create an online self is comparably less straightforward. What it means to represent self is socially, politically, and historically situated. That is, while people have choices in deciding how to represent themselves in online spaces, deciding what is appropriate and acceptable to present depends on the context of representation. Writing oneself into an online being can be quite challenging. Again, consider my notes about my decisions regarding how to represent myself as a researcher:

> Now with a new picture representing me, I navigate my way to the class biographies — a forum page, where people can create their profile pages to introduce themselves to others — and start writing myself into being. Although I have already taken many online courses through this medium during my course work and written my online self a few times before, I am struggling with how to represent myself, particularly as a researcher. While I acknowledge that such concerns are not exclusive to doing research on the Internet, I find myself unsure of my self-representation about my identification. How should I introduce myself? What aspects of myself and my personality should I put forward? How can I make sure that they understand who I am? What is the best way to create these relationships?
>
> Frustrated, I log out.
>
> I log back in later at that night and finish what I started earlier on in the day. I continue editing my note and introduce myself as I write who I think I am, or who I think I want to be known as. I try to represent myself as close as I can be to myself; I want others to know me and understand my research. I am not here because I am interested in playing phantasies or exploring other identities.[1] I am here because I am conducting research. My online self is finally alive.

While these are my own struggles of creating an online self, I shall demonstrate in this chapter that such a process is by no means exclusive to me. The rest of this chapter examines how the participants in this book created their online self and managed impressions with respect to macro-level Discourses in online spaces. Specifically, I shall analyse the interplay between self-representation, identification, and impression management with respect to macro-level societal Discourses. I illustrate how impression management is shaped by the dynamics of race and ethnicity, with a focus on whiteness.

3.1 The art of creating an online self

In the case of online education, a digital body is created when one registers for the online course. The process continues as people type in some information about themselves in profile pages.[2] The profile pages in the two online courses were semi-structured. The instructor provided three questions (asking students to offer personal traits, strengths, and previous experiences); however, people were free to answer (or not to answer) those questions in any way they wanted – with no limitations of word count.

Despite the fact that creating a profile page is an open-ended task in terms of creativity, the process of creating an online self is not arbitrary. As I will illustrate, individuals simply want to be identified as "good students". However, what it means to be a good student, and the qualities that convey the image of a good student, have different meanings for different individuals. Yet, participants in these online courses tend to highlight three aspects of themselves as they convey the image of a good student: social life, professional work, and academic success. In most cases, these three personal aspects are used in concert for impression management. In this section, I focus on how online selves create a social context. In the next section, I focus on the social-political aspects of impression management and analyse what is at stake in impression management.

The desire to be seen as interesting in social life, caring or helpful in personal life, successful in professional work, and competitive in academic studies is a challenging task that has to be carefully managed in creating an online self. Take Johanne for instance. She strongly focuses on her social life. Her profile picture with a big smile on her face accompanies the following text:

> I am a first year PhD student and I recently graduated in June from City University's Master of Education program. . . . I have a bubbly personality. I know that I am always smiling and laughing with my family and friends. At first, I am quiet because I like to observe, but once I get comfortable, I'll come out of my shell and then it becomes difficult to keep me quiet. I noticed that I enjoy creating remix videos, whether it is about a family vacation or on course readings, I find that these videos help to further articulate ideas in a cheery and refreshing way. . . . I like being able to help people in my own way (whether it's editing a peer's paper or cutting for hours to help teacher friends prepare class activities), so they can complete their tasks – I'm there. Outside of school I enjoy hanging out with my family and friends, doing yoga, listening to music, scrapbooking, traveling, cooking, and watching my favourite TV shows.

While we get very little about Johanne's academic or professional life, her online self suggests that she is highly active and outgoing in her social life.

Johanne's online self-reveals clues about her personality traits. Indeed, when I met Johanne in person for interviews, I observed her "bubbly personality". She was energetic, positive, cheerful, and smiling at all times. By creating her online self as personally and socially desirable, Johanne conveys the message that she is "there" when her peers need her.

There seems to be no predefined formula for how much and where to focus in terms of personality attributes. While some people may prefer to reflect more on their academic success or personal traits, others stress their social interests and hobbies. It is a delicate balance that each person has to figure out to convey the image of a good student. Courtney's online self is more of an academic. With a friendly smile in her picture, she writes herself into online being:

> I am a first year PhD student. I have just finished my Master's here in this department, and I am looking forward to continuing my journey. One of my favourite parts of grad school is taking courses! So I am really excited to be here and to learn from you all. I have a lifelong interest in education – I have taught Elementary school (Grade 6) and have also been a High School Visual Arts teacher. One of my passions is technology use for education – particularly in school settings. The research projects that I take part in with my lab all involve developing innovative technologies for Elementary Science classrooms, to connect kids with kids, and to allow them to share their ideas and findings with each other. I am not sure exactly where my PhD interests lie, but I may be interested in pursuing location or gesture-based technologies within these contexts. . . . I guess I would also describe myself as "tenacious" (some might say stubborn!!). But basically, I work really hard, and keep working until I reach my goals. This trait is manifest in my academic work as well as in my personal life.

Compared to Johanne, Courtney provides almost no information about her social life but foregrounds her academic success. Despite selecting a different aspect of herself to highlight, Courtney does what Johanne does: convey the message that she is a good student. As a "tenacious" student, Courtney's online self suggests that her peers can rely on her when it comes to group work.

Along with social interests and academic work, profession and career highlights are used for representing oneself in mediated spaces. Amy underscores her professional work when she creates her online self:

> I've been doing my MEd online on a part time basis over the past few years. I've been teaching English as a second language for the past six years – and have had the opportunity to work in Tibet, Saudi Arabia, Taiwan, and Pakistan. I'm in Korea this year living at a temple and teaching English to Buddhist nuns. It's a bit hectic as I'm also developing the curriculum – but definitely an amazing experience. I also have a lot of empathy which I

find really helpful in my teaching practice, particularly with Second Language Learners where language anxiety can be a huge barrier to learning. I've also learned from previous courses that online communication can be really helpful in overcoming this anxiety – one of the reasons I need to get more comfortable with implementing these kinds of approaches in my classroom. I made a wiki for a facilitation assignment which went really well but am now in the process of redoing the blogs I set up for my students due some mysterious technical problems. It's been frustrating, but I am determined to learn how to integrate technology in a meaningful way into my practice.

Amy gives very limited information about her academic interests or social life but explains her professional success in detail. Of course, one might infer an interesting social life as a result of her broad travels. Indeed, after our second interview, Amy and I had a long off-the-record conversation about her international experience as a teacher and she stated that she – after our conversation – wished that she included more of her social experience in her profile page. Regardless, by putting herself forward as a dedicated and considerate teacher, Amy's online self implies that she is highly professional (particularly given that this is a course in the field of education) and knowledgeable.

While the three excerpts above illustrate how individuals create online selves by using their social, professional, and academic life realities, it does not mean that they use these categories in an isolated fashion. Participants use the combination of these categories to a certain extent and emphasise two or more aspects of their offline realities. Take Jeff, for example. His online self includes aspects of both a teacher and a student:

> I am a full-time PhD student in another department. . . . This is my first online course in this institution. I taught EFL in Asia and Europe for 16 years and am still adjusting to being a full-time student. . . . I have integrated social media into blended EFL and EAP courses. I use Twitter, Facebook, LinkedIn, and academia.edu as my personal learning network (PLN) and encourage my students to cultivate their own PLNs. . . . I am looking forward to enhancing my understanding of online learning (surprise emoticon).

Jeff's online self in many ways is in between Amy and Courtney. Similar to Amy, Jeff highlights his international teaching career while at the same time, similar to Courtney, he articulates that he treats his learning as a journey. In addition to these two aspects, Jeff wants his online self to be known as funny – or as a joker, as he stated in one of our interviews. In his profile page, he writes that procrastination is one of his positive traits. When I asked Jeff about this joke, he explained that he did not have any idea of what to write as a positive personal trait, and thus decided to joke on how many hours he spent writing

42 Writing oneself into online being

up his profile page. According to Jeff, his profile picture also reflects his fun approach to his online self:

> I was six years old in that picture. I was in school and I have lots of books behind me. It was done for the purpose of picture. I didn't want to have my current image up there. Also, it signified to myself that this is a new subject area to me, and I wanted to feel that I am back to school. It is like . . . a reminder that I am back to school.

While I do not get Jeff's joke about his profile picture, he certainly put much effort in creating his online self as a fun person. For Jeff, being a good student means to be an experienced teacher and a dedicated student, who is also a funny person in his personal life.

Personal traits are also common in creating online selves. Sydney's online self represents more of her personal traits than anything else:

> I am a full-time student working on my Master of Education degree. I graduated last year from Lakeview University. I love learning, being in an educational space and being a "professional student" as many would say. I have been told that I am a very warm and friendly individual. It is rare to see me without a smile on my face. I am also very sensitive to the needs of others. I am a very organized individual especially when it comes to work or school. I am also very focused and determined. Once I set my mind to something, I will work very hard until I achieve it. I love spending my spare time with my family. I also love reading and in particular I enjoy psychological thrillers. In addition, I enjoy singing, yoga, and going out on the four-wheeler. Animals are another passion of mine. I volunteer at a local animal shelter and spend as much time there as possible.

She highlights her online self as warm, sensitive, and caring: qualities that everyone looks for in others. Her online self is not only friendly but also very organised and determined. She is socially active and volunteers. Clearly, Sydney's online self conveys the notion that she is someone that would enjoy learning from and with others.

When asked, participants suggested that they spent time and put an effort to carefully create online selves. They did try to convey certain messages about themselves. Determining what to write, which information to put forward, and choosing the right picture – definitely with a smile – is an important task in creating the online self. Some people, however, do not upload their pictures but use an image that is by default assigned by the system. Yet, they still carefully write themselves into online beings. Gulsum for example used the daisy picture. When I asked her why she did not upload her own picture, she explained:

> I didn't have a picture ready to upload. I am not interested in [that] anyway. . . . But I don't think I have a picture of myself. I mean I have family

pictures, with my kids and with my husband. I could have got a picture scanned and uploaded . . . but, um, . . . I mean it is just time. I work full-time, I study full-time, I have three kids . . . so, um, . . . it was just one more thing to do and it was too much. . . . But I changed my picture from a shoe[3] to a daisy. I cannot be a shoe, right?

Gulsum claims that she did not have the time or motivation to upload her picture. Yet, she cared sufficiently to change her profile picture from shoe to daisy. When prompted, Gulsum replied that shoes are culturally inappropriate because they are accepted as unclean, and thus she changed her profile picture. Furthermore, she took her time to consider what to write in her profile and how to represent herself. I was puzzled by Gulsum's attitude towards her profile picture. In my interviews with her, I reminded Gulsum of my observation about her picture and discussed the motivation behind her decisions. Since I am interested in understanding the effects of macro-level Discourses on individuals' online education experiences, I was curious whether her decisions were shaped by social dynamics. Gulsum strongly denied the possibility of any extrinsic social pressure[4] (though she believed the shoe was culturally inappropriate) but insisted that it was a matter of time commitment.

Although Gulsum does not have a picture of herself, her online self conveys much information about her: she is a teacher, a busy mother, and a successful student:

> I am pursuing an MEd degree and this is hopefully my last semester :) I worked as a business consultant for three years in Egypt before moving to Canada with my husband in 2001. I run a Montessori School in [a suburban neighbourhood] from toddlers to Grade 3. I worked as a Montessori teacher for four years and still teach to lower elementary for the past three years. Since January 2008, I have been working as an instructor at [a private college], offering accredited Montessori teachers' training programs. I have three children and I changed my career to become a teacher because I love children. . . . I am a hard worker and love to be around people in general and children in particular. . . . In my "spare" time I like traveling, cooking, and learning new languages (I speak four: Arabic, English, French, and German) and I hope to learn Spanish.

Gulsum decided to represent herself as a hard worker, both in her personal and professional life. However, I was not able to think of her with the same sense of reality as I felt for the others, simply because she did not have her picture in her profile page. When there is a personal picture in a profile, I believe I am able to get a very good sense of who the person is behind that profile (I was not surprised by who I met for interviews). Nevertheless, I was not able to truly imagine Gulsum in flesh and blood. How she really looked was a mystery to me until the day I met her for the very first time on a very cold night for an interview.

44 Writing oneself into online being

A picture is worth a thousand words is a famous expression, referring to the power of visual representation in communication. In line with this adage, research indicates that profile pictures are significantly correlated with affection and social attraction in online spaces (Floridi, 2012; Walther, 2007). My interviews yielded similar results. When I asked my participants how they made sense of people without personal pictures, they all posited that they had negative attitudes against such individuals. "I cannot make sense of them, so I move on" said Sydney. Jeff articulated that he felt "sorry for them" because he believed "there must be something wrong with them". Johanne's attitude was also negative. She suggested that people without pictures "creep her out". She added: "we are not going to be friends if you don't have your picture. I cannot have relationship with you". By contrast, Gulsum suggested that she did not sense any negative attitude against her. Rather, she believed that her peers were "very warm" to her.

Profile pages in online education are aimed at introducing people to one another, assuming that people do not already know each other from other courses or from daily life beyond school. While the person behind a profile may or may not be known to others, online selves are crafted to explain the self to strangers, motivating individuals to carefully consider which aspects or features to highlight in their self-representation. This does not mean that people write their profiles for complete strangers or write them with no sense of potential readership. People are aware that others in the online space are also students with whom they will study together. People acknowledge others' presence and address them in their profiles. Courtney salutes her new friends and sends her "best wishes to all for a successful term!"; Amy expresses her excitement for sharing the space with others and states that "it's really great to be here and [she is] looking forward to getting to know [her] peers better during this course!"; and Gulsum indicates her willingness to work together as she is "looking forward to learning with and from all [of her] friends and [she] thanks everyone for the support in advance :)". Acknowledging the presence of others, however, goes beyond mere salutations or expressions of good will but shapes the dynamics around how one represents the self.

3.2 Impression management in the online context

Typing the self into online existence is not a random performance nor does the process of creating online self occur in a void. The ways in which people represent themselves and engage with each other is a socially situated process. That is, our daily life is spent in the immediate presence of others and the process of impression management is enacted once individuals – for whatever reason – come into one another's immediate presence (Goffman, 1983). The same is true for online education, where people always act in the presence of others. As I shall illustrate below, my participants suggest that in online spaces, deciding how to write about oneself, what information to reveal, and which

Writing oneself into online being 45

picture to upload (or whether to upload at all) are all dependent upon the presence of others in the context.

Johanne explained what it means to represent herself in mediated spaces and how she typed herself into an online being:

> Obviously, you want to look good. You don't want to look like all academic and nerd. You obviously want to look good too . . . um. . . . You want to present yourself in a particular manner. You have to choose traits that get looked at or complimented [in order] to attract people. So that's what I was doing. I didn't want to be boring. So, what I did was that I added some of my . . ., um, things like . . . I actually added pictures of where I travelled . . . . um. . . . So, when I was just doing this, my goal was just to make my classmates engage with me because it is just hard to engage with people in online learning spaces. I want to be approachable and look like enthusiastic. You know what I mean? Also, you want to advertise that you are a good student. So, you kind of want to choose things that compliment your online learning aspect because I think you have to have traits for online learning that are different from [those] face-to-face ones. So, I wanted to be seen as approachable, friendly, and, um, helpful. I didn't want to come off as . . . um, I don't know, I didn't want to come off as a boring person or, um, as crazy picky. I was thinking what people would think of me and how they react to me. You don't want to come off as hoity-toity or pompous. You know . . . (laughs) that's actually a Caribbean saying. You don't want to come off like that but [want to be seen as] friendly. I was just thinking advertising myself. Advertising all of my academic accomplishments. That's also part of who you are. People want to know what your background is. You know what I mean? You want to make yourself look good. When creating my profile, I was keeping my peers in mind, as well as the instructor. So, I was reading it from my peers' point of view and my instructor's point of view. I was asking [myself] how it would look like or appear to them; how would the virtual Johanne appear to them. That's what it was in my mind.

The process Johanne went through captures and reflects the essence of what Goffman (1959) defined as impression management: in order to look good, one has to consider the context and represent himself or herself in a manner that attracts people. Yet, what it means to look good in the context of online education is an open-ended question.

Impression management is part of everyday life in mediated spaces and it is performed through and negotiated by profile pages. For example, Johanne explains that she wants to "look good" and tries to "make a good impression"; therefore, she "advertise[s]" herself in her profile page. The process that Johanne defines as advertisement is at the heart of impression management. Making the right advertisement to the right audience is important: what content to display

46 Writing oneself into online being

in online selves is contextual, determined by the space, social situation, and people (boyd, 2008). In the case of online education, people similarly keep their intended audience in mind when they represent themselves. For Johanne, advertising herself means "to make [her] classmates engage with [her]" by choosing "traits that get looked at or complimented". She posits that when creating her online profile, she keeps her peers in mind in order to decide how to represent herself as a good student: "I was thinking what people would think of me and how they react to me". Thus, Johanne considers how to represent herself based on the context in which she enacts.

In online education, people are aware that the audience is limited to the other students (along with the instructor) in the space. Therefore, people craft their online selves particularly for the other students in the same online space. For example, Courtney says: "Did I spent a lot of time in creating my profile, yes. Did I concern how others will see me, yes. But I wanted to be seen as a good student; a student who is on a learning journey". For Courtney, being on a learning journey means being "tenacious": "I work really hard and keep working until I reach my goals. This trait is manifest in my academic work". Courtney knows that her online peers are her audience and she sends a message to them: "I am really excited to be here and to learn from you all".

Indeed, the notion of "being on a learning journey" is manifest in many online selves I examined. It is a common way by which people try to make connections with other students in the course. Devran, for example, postulates that she is "excited about this course and looks forward to learning with everyone". She continues and represents herself as a good "team worker": "I believe that I am more creative and productive in a team". In this sense, representing oneself as "being on a learning journey" is a strategy to recognise other students in the course and situate oneself in relation to those around them.

Because the audience is other students in the course, representing oneself as a good student is a common concern regarding impression management in online education. Take, for example, Sofia's explanation of what it means to represent the self to other students in online education spaces:

> I knew that my profile was the first impression that other students are going to have of me. So, I wanted to make sure that everything flowed properly. I wanted to come across as academic, I suppose. And I added all about my personality as well. I wanted to make sure that I was coming off as a good student but also friendly; so, I was putting up my personal aspects. I like to include emoticons here and there . . . (laughs). I think emoticons help them to see me who I am as a student, as a person.

And when asked what it means to "come off as a good student", she further elaborates:

> I wanted to be taken seriously as a student and I was like . . . this is my first impression . . . so, I wanted to make a good impression. Who wants

to make a bad impression, anyway? It is awful. So, I wanted to make sure that . . . you know . . . when people read it, they kind of get a sense of who I am as a student and person. I wanted them to be comfortable talking to me and responding to my profile. I was concerned how people will see me and it is a pretty normal thing, right?

As Sofia's explanation illustrates, representing oneself to other students means that one has to be a "good student", "serious academic", and yet be friendly and smiley at the same time. Similarly, for Kate, being a good student means being organised and helpful:

For me, I organise things and be precise. I am really good at organising my studying materials or . . . um . . . and I like to help out people and I give [them] examples and help them understand [the readings] better.

What it means to be a good student, therefore, is something that students negotiate in online education; people try to impress each other as they seek to present the perfect combination of their traits as a student and as a person.

In online selves I examined, my participants think of their online selves as entities wherein they can utilise and make evident their various qualities. One's skills, abilities, interests, accomplishments, and other traits or qualities, then, become means by which people negotiate their first impressions. "Your online self is a combination of different traits", says Sydney, and continues:

coming off as a serious academic was my priority but I also wanted to include aspects from my personality. Also, I didn't want to be like . . . "oh, look at everything I have done so far. Look how successful I am". It is like . . . all flashy flashy . . . you know what I mean? I didn't want to do that.

Others have different approaches in representing themselves. For example, while Johanne's online self is all about her personality and her social interests beyond school, Courtney's online self is strict to her academic achievements with just a touch of reference to her social interests.

Personal traits, interests, and qualities are common means by which the participants utilise their online selves. Even though the online space in which I conducted this research does not provide many technological options for customising the way profile pages look (e.g. changing the background, layout, or colours), the participants I interviewed believe that their profiles are customised and unique to them. For example, Johanne thinks "personalising is the most important thing in creating the profile pages". She further explains how she personalised her online self:

I wanted to put what I like to do out of the school. So, I put my family and friends, and places I travelled. I put the TV shows I like to watch. I personalised [my profile] so others actually can see who I am and what I do beyond the class.

48 Writing oneself into online being

Reflecting personal traits, qualities, and interests not only allows people to customise their online selves but also serves as means by which people develop a sense of commonality, a sense that is vital for people to engage with each other. Familiarity and similarity are crucial for establishing communication, forming relationships, and developing solidarity among people (Goffman, 1983). This was also true for online relationships. Similarities and commonalities were the first thing people try to find when they look at others' profiles. Sydney, for example, says:

> I was trying to find similarities between me and others . . . um, because I wasn't sure who were going to be in my class. You don't know anything about them. I had no clue. So, I was just looking for similarities . . . you know . . . to start up a conversation with people and make connections. Similarities and things in common. That is the first thing I was looking at.

When I asked her if she was able to make any real connection, she nodded and further explained: "I found Johanne to be very similar to me and I responded to her and I said 'oh, look, we have similarities' and we eventually ended up as [being] close friends". Indeed, Johanne also mentioned how she ended up being a close friend with Sydney as they realised their similarities. Johanne further explained to me how she was trying to find similarities with her peers so that she could make connections with them:

> If I find anything to connect with people, either for social, academic, or professional aspects, then I will respond [to that person] and say "hey". And, if I cannot find that connection, I just don't respond to them.

The fact that people use their similarities to make social connections was evident in their responses to others. In my interviews, the participants articulated that they looked for similar interests or experiences they have with others and asked more questions or offered further explanation to deepen the social encounters.

By and large, online selves create the first impression and set the tone for the communication process. For instance, Johanne thinks of her profile page as "like the first impression you give to your peers as well as your instructor". When I ask her why she thinks of profile pages as the first impression, she explains:

> because [the profile] is, um . . . kind of . . . um, going to set the tone [for] who you are, you are going to be, and you want to be in [online] classroom. And if you set the wrong tone, um, you can turn people off.

Sydney thinks similarly; for her, profile pages are places, where people introduce themselves to others for the first time. I ask her what it means to introduce oneself in mediated spaces. She replies:

Um, I basically thought about meeting with someone else for the first time in face to face. It is like . . . introducing yourself. It is the first impression that people have about you. So I wanted to make it . . . um, I wanted to sound good and you know . . . I tried to incorporate as much as I can about myself.

Profile pages, in this sense, provide means from which social life originates in online education spaces.

While online selves create the tone and make the first impression, maintaining that tone and impression is an ongoing process. People have to perform in ways concordant with the representations offered in the profiles. This does not mean that individuals have to constantly update their profile pages to manage their impressions; rather, they have to perform the qualities and abilities they claimed when they engage with each other in weekly discussions. As Nalini explains:

everyone says that they are a good [student] but . . . you can only keep on that impression if it is true. You have to be who you are in your profile; otherwise people just don't care what you [said you] are in the profile.

According to Nalini, impression management is not a one-time performance but an ongoing process; a process people have to repeat every day to sustain their impressions.

The role of online selves in online spaces can be understood both at personal and social levels. At the personal level, online selves provide opportunities for individuals to reify their qualities, traits, and interests in online spaces. In other words, online selves allow individuals to manage and negotiate their identification to make their experiences more meaningful and personalised. For example, Courtney says:

You want to give people a little bit of information about yourself, so that they can get to know you a little. And because they will know you, they will be a little bit comfortable talking to you. It makes the learning personal, you know. It is not like, . . . like, all faceless technology that seems cold [but] you are creating a sense of human touch. I really revealed myself. So, for me, it was about having my online . . . it was like being alive online.

At the social level, profile pages allow individuals to make sense of the context in which they operate and of their peers with whom they engage. For example, Sydney says:

I think that it establishes a sense of community rather than just being tossed into the environment without knowing who your peers are. It just helps make connections and helps make sense of who you are talking to, which I think foster discussion and even collaboration.

50 Writing oneself into online being

Consequently, because profile pages have both personal and social aspects, they allow individuals to situate themselves in their context. Thus, profile pages become central means for individuals to manage their impressions.

Taken together, what it means to represent the self in online spaces seems not so different from what it means to represent the self in daily life. The mediated space provides the participants with opportunities for reflecting the best aspects of themselves. In order to highlight their best selves, people negotiate their representations and try to impress the others in the online space. Individuals I interviewed suggested that they explored those who were around them, observed others, and created their online selves while they explicitly expressed themselves, and in return were impressed by others. Consequently, behind social engagements and interactions in mediated spaces, there is a dialectic understanding stemming from the impressions given to, or taken by, others. The following section discusses how this dialectic understanding works with respect to Discourses and what is at stake in the process of impression management.

3.3 Representation of self in online education

When people create their online selves, they do not create a whole personality that is totally different from who they are in their daily lives; rather, they reproduce themselves in a digital space (Hardey, 2002). For example, Kate says, "I am who I am and my online self is the same". Similarly, Nalini posits, "I tried to stay true to what I put in my profile and I was myself, so, um, . . . um, my profile was me". Courtney is concerned with being misunderstood as to who she is: "I don't want to be misunderstood, misinterpreted. So, I take a long time to make sure that who I am is clear. That's the main thing". Devran says that she wanted to "make sure that she is going to be taken as who she is in her daily life". Sydney articulates that she wanted to be known as who she actually is: "I wanted them to get a general sense of who I am . . . like . . . like they would know me in a face-to-face space". She continues: "I think my profile is just reflecting who I am in the real world". While Kate, Nalini, Courtney, Devran, and Sydney offer essentialist[5] and deterministic[6] perspectives in comparing their online selves with "who they are" in the "real world", they point out that the impressions they convey online are similar to the impressions they convey face to face. In other words, they all suggest that what is at stake in their face-to-face impression management is also at stake in their online impression management.

Online selves, therefore, not only help individuals to reproduce themselves in online spaces with respect to daily life realities but also allow them to bring macro-level societal Discourses in online education, whether intentionally or not. Accordingly, Discourses and online selves are dialectically related: Discourses shape online selves and online selves in turn reproduce the very same Discourses. While other Discourses are also at play,[7] in this book, I focus on Discourses of whiteness to analyse impression management.

Writing oneself into online being 51

Discourses of whiteness refer to the set of societal privileges that are granted to those who are identified as white (McIntosh, 2003). Such privileges include greater social status, access to everyday goods (e.g. food, health protection, safer neighbourhoods, police and fire protection), access to quality education, and basic civil liberties (i.e. freedom to move, buy, work, play, and speak freely) (Crenshaw, Gotanda, Peller, & Thomas, 1995). The notion of white privilege implies that whites benefit from these privileges beyond those commonly experienced by non-whites in the same social, political, cultural, educational, or economic spaces (Delgado & Stefancic, 2012). The concept of whiteness, therefore, denotes otherwise non-obvious privileges that whites have; or put differently, it denotes non-obvious racial or ethnic bias or prejudice non-whites experience. According to this understanding, whiteness is a property (intellectual, cultural, or legal) with an intrinsic value that must be protected (Harris, 1993). The concept of whiteness is not a biological or phenotypical (i.e. skin colour) category. Rather, it is a discursive construction and, as any discursive construction, it can be reinvented, modified, or discarded. As social construction, Discourses of whiteness provide sets of norms against which all non-whites are judged, measured, and positioned.

In the online courses I studied, Discourses of whiteness manifested themselves through the process of impression management; particularly, through the negotiations of what constitutes a good student. By highlighting their achievements, traits, desires, hobbies, and qualities, the participants reproduced their online selves in line with the white norms of desire and intelligence. This does not mean that non-whites are unintelligent or undesirable nor does it mean that non-whites want to be seen as white. Rather, it means that by highlighting their achievements and success in line with the Discourses of whiteness, non-whites try to claim their legitimacy, their right to be in the online course. Through impression management, non-whites in this study negotiate their status of belonging to their community. For example, Gulsum had to manage and negotiate her identification in order to be accepted as an equal participant. Gulsum believed that she is not accepted as intelligent; therefore, she was worried that her peers did not want to work with her:

> You want to, um . . . um, you want people to know who you are. You are trying to put the positive side [of yourself] and even though you might put negative things, you just rephrase them, um, you . . . you sugar-coat them, in a sense. And, um, you want to put the achievements so that, um, . . . you want to put your achievements but not limited to academic life but also professional life, your working life. By reading my achievements, um, . . . so, like people say, um, "ok, I can work with you for group projects". So, my aim was to . . . to make people know the good side of me; so that my achievements can overshadow any judgement that they might make [of me]. Like, anything to help them . . . like . . . um, for instance, you know because of my name, I am not from here. So, when you see me,

52   Writing oneself into online being

my achievements can be overshadowed by the fact that some of my peers might be biased [against me]. So, you want to represent yourself in a way that it intrigues people to know more about you.

Gulsum thought that it was necessary for her to represent herself as competent and rigorous because she believed her peers had biases against her just because she is not identified as White – even though she is officially white according to the Canadian census. In specific, Gulsum worried about her name and believed that she would be identified as non-white, and thus accepted as not intelligent. According to Gulsum, intelligence and success were associated with being identified as white. In other words, intelligence and success were the property of whiteness. What is at stake for Gulsum is her inclusion or exclusion from her community. Impression management is a process of survival that I will explore in detail in Chapters 4 and 5.

Caught in the white interpretive filter, those who are identified as non-white believed that they have to demonstrate that they can be as intelligent and desirable as whites are assumed to be. For example, Nalini used impression management to convey that she is as good as her peers:

> my name was there, right? So, [my peers] guess . . . um, they assume that I am brown, and I have a different name, so I am not Canadian or white.

Later, Nalini continued:

> I was trying to put in some stuff that will make people think that I am a good student because I wanted people to consider me for homework and for the final project. I wanted to attract people so they would . . . so that they would consider working with me. I wanted my online profile to be intelligent because this is the only chance that I can explain . . . that I can make sure that I am taken as intelligent. Because I am as intelligent as [my peers] are.

Nalini articulated that it was necessary for her to represent herself as intelligent and successful because she believed that her name reveals that she is not white. She deemed it necessary to explicitly convey her intelligence to counteract biases that would otherwise cast her as less intelligent than others.

For Devran, impression management was a chance to prove her academic success. Devran is a PhD student from Turkey and she received her previous degrees from a Turkish university. She posits that "because [she] didn't get [her] degrees from a Canadian or an American institution, [her] success might not be fully understood", even though her "university is one of the top universities in Turkey". In order to convey an impression that she is a successful student, Devran says that she explained how her accomplishments would look in the Canadian context. Indeed, in her profile page, she wrote: "Before I came to

Writing oneself into online being   53

Canada, I worked as a research and teaching assistant in my university. I had responsibilities of teaching courses and grading students. It is like being a lecturer here in [departments name]".

Identified as non-white, Gulsum, Nalini, and Devran believed that their intelligence and success were devalued, under constant threat, or subject to negotiation at all times. Devaluation of perspectives, values, and qualities of non-whites are how Discourses of whiteness operate (Kincheloe, 2010). Since the normative standards of intelligence rely on cultural difference between whites and non-whites, Discourses of whiteness create a hierarchy that non-whites cannot overcome.

3.4 Conclusion: reproducing the self, reproducing the Discourses

How people represent themselves and manage impressions in mediated learning spaces can be thought of as what Butler (1990) calls performative acts. With respect to gender and sexuality, the theory of performative acts suggests that gender norms are culturally constructed through the repetition of performances. While Butler particularly refers to gendered norms, the theory can be applied to other identity manifestations in mediated spaces (Van Doorn, 2009). People perform their online selves by embodying an online existence, managing impressions, and reproducing their identities through what Butler calls performative repetitions.

Performing the online self not only embodies people but also situates and contextualises them in relation to those around them. The online selves place individuals in particular temporal and spatial relationships and cultural practices. In other words, by creating and performing online selves, people bring material and symbolic dynamics of their daily life into mediated environments. Such material and symbolic conditions, then, become means by which people try to impress each other in order to fulfil their desires. Therefore, the performance of self in online spaces reproduces macro-level societal Discourses under which people operate in their daily lives. Consequently, self-representation and impression management in mediated spaces create what Foucault (1978) calls a *discursive regime*,[8] in which people create sets of social norms and rules, and in return self-monitor to follow such norms and rules. For Butler (1990), the discursive regime affects the meanings of what is acceptable and appropriate; therefore, people are not free performing the self and in most cases the self is performed without one being conscious of it. The discursive regime is also manifest in online experiences. When people perform their selves in online spaces, they do not enact freely or randomly, but are culturally constrained by and within discourses; while certain performances are allowed, others are prohibited.

For online education, the discursive regime is manifest in decisions regarding who can be included in or excluded from the asynchronous discussions

54 Writing oneself into online being

and learning community at large. Particularly, the discursive regime affects the norms and values of what aspects of the self are acceptable, allowed, and appropriate to represent in order to become included in the learning community. In sociopolitical terms, online selves can be seen as means to negotiate who has rights, responsibilities, power, and control over others. While there is no direct or material domination between whites and non-whites, data presented in this chapter suggest that non-whites are dominated by white people's perspectives through the Discourses of whiteness. Political aspects can be seen as the process of legitimising who can speak with what authority. As data in this chapter show, non-white participants try to claim their legitimacy by conveying impressions that they are as good, as successful, and as desirable as whites. With the pictures they upload, with the words they type, people claim their right to be in the online learning space and their right to be included in the community.

In this chapter, I have shown that online spaces do not disembody people or decontextualise social engagements. By analysing what it means to represent the self and what it means to negotiate impressions in mediated spaces, I have demonstrated that people use material resources available to them in their daily-life realities when they dialogically create a shared social reality. Finally, I have argued that as people perform their selves, they create a discursive regime in mediated spaces. In the next chapter, I explore how people navigate in and through this discursive regime.

Notes

1 Unlike online education environments, in online environments like MUDs (i.e. World of Warcraft), participants do not need to accurately reflect who they are. People usually go to such environments just to "play with their identities", "escape from their bodies", and explore their "second selves" (Turkle, 2005). Indeed, such spaces are built to allow imagined identities and simulate various phantasies (Sundén, 2003). More often than not, people bend their identities just to explore what it means to be like someone else. For example, the "Alex Affair" is a famously known story about gender bending. In this story, a male psychiatrist pretends to be a woman in a women-only chat room and he soon realises how intimate his patients can get with "Joan" – his fake woman character. See Turkle (1997) for more details. Therefore, the selves created in MUDs are not necessarily "real" in a sense that I argue in this book. In online learning, identity bending does not happen as often – indeed, I was not able to identify a single study about it – since existing identities are central in learning spaces.
2 There is no standardised name or application in the practice of online education. In different online education spaces, a profile page might be called by a different name. A profile page in an online education space is similar to those profiles in social network sites but less detailed and less complicated when compared to them. One of the biggest differences between a profile in social network and online education is the option of "friending" with others. In online education, people are friends by default and are already a member of a learning community. Yet another big difference is the maintenance of the profile pages: while profiles in social networks are more dynamic and more regularly updated, profiles in online education are somewhat static; in most cases are created once at the beginning of the course without being changed.

Writing oneself into online being 55

3 Just another system picture that may be randomly assigned to a person. For Gulsum, a shoe is, somehow, culturally inappropriate to represent oneself.
4 However, as I will illustrate in Chapters 4 and 5, Gulsum is aware of Discourses and explains in her own words how she positioned herself with respect to Discourses of whiteness.
5 As I argued in Chapter 2, essentialist perspectives suggest that self is a static and stable entity, regardless of the context in which self is enacted.
6 As I argued in Chapter 2, deterministic perspectives suggest that online and offline are two distinct modes of being. However, I argued that online and offline cannot be distinguished clearly and that online does not mean not real.
7 See, for example, Sundén (2003) and Haraway (1991) for gendered construction of self; Byrne (2008) for racial construction of self; Burston, Dyer-Witheford, and Hearn (2010) for social class-based construction of self.
8 The discursive regime is also acknowledged by Goffman; however, he refers them as "establishment" (1959) and, later, as "frames" (1983).

References

boyd, d. (2008). Why youth ♥ social network sites: The role of networked publics in teenage social life. In D. Buckingham (Ed.), *Youth, identity, and digital media* (pp. 119–142). Cambridge, MA: MIT Press Journals.

Burston, J., Dyer-Witheford, N., & Hearn, A. (2010). Digital labour: Workers, authors, citizens. *Ephemera, 10*, 214–221.

Butler, J. (1990). *Gender trouble: Feminism and the subversion of identity*. New York, NY: Routledge.

Byrne, D. N. (2008). The future of (the) "race": Identity, discourse, and the rise of computer-mediated public spheres. In A. Everett (Ed.), *Learning race and ethnicity: Youth and digital media* (pp. 15–38). Cambridge, MA: MIT Press.

Crenshaw, K., Gotanda, N., Peller, G., & Thomas, K. (1995). *Critical race theory: The key writings that formed the movement*. New York, NY: The New Press.

Delgado, R., & Stefancic, J. (2012). *Critical race theory: An introduction* (2nd ed.). New York, NY: New York University Press.

Floridi, L. (2012). Technologies of the self. *Philosophy & Technology, 25*(3), 271–273. doi:10.1007/s13347-012-0083-6

Foucault, M. (1978). *The history of sexuality, Vol. 1: An introduction* (R. Hurley, Trans.). New York, NY: Vintage.

Goffman, E. (1959). *The presentation of self in everyday life*. New York, NY: Anchor Books.

Goffman, E. (1983). The interaction order: American Sociological Association, 1982 presidential address. *American Sociological Review, 48*(1), 1–17. doi:10.2307/2095141

Haraway, D. J. (1991). *Simians, cyborgs, and women: The reinvention of nature*. New York, NY: Routledge.

Hardey, M. (2002). Life beyond the screen: Embodiment and identity through the internet. *The Sociological Review, 50*(4), 570–585. doi:10.1111/1467-954x.00399

Harris, C. I. (1993). Whiteness as property. *Harvard Law Review, 106*(8), 1707–1791. doi:10.2307/1341787

Kincheloe, J. L. (2010). White studies research, critical. In C. Kridel (Ed.), *Encyclopedia of curriculum studies* (pp. 940–944). Thousands Oak, CA: Sage Publications.

McIntosh, P. (2003). White privilege and male privilege: A personal account of coming to see correspondences through work in women's studies. In M. S. Kimmel & A. L. Ferber (Eds.), *Privilege: A reader* (pp. 147–160). New York, NY: Basic Books.

Sundén, J. (2003). *Material virtualities: Approaching online textual embodiment.* New York, NY: Peter Lang Publishing.

Turkle, S. (1997). *Life on the screen: Identity in the age of the internet.* New York, NY: Simon & Schuster.

Turkle, S. (2005). *The second self: Computers and the human spirit* (20th Anniversary ed.). Cambridge, MA: MIT Press.

Van Doorn, N. (2009). The ties that bind: The networked performance of gender, sexuality and friendship on MySpace. *New Media & Society, 12*(4), 583–602. doi:10.1177/1461444809342766

Walther, J. B. (2007). Selective self-presentation in computer-mediated communication: Hyperpersonal dimensions of technology, language, and cognition. *Computers in Human Behavior, 23*(5), 2538–2557. doi:10.1016/j.chb.2006.05.002

Chapter 4

Hierarchy of privilege
Self as curriculum of diversity and otherness

The previous chapter showed how online selves allow people to write themselves into online beings and negotiate identification. Since Discourses define and determine social practice, I argued that online selves embody material realities of the broader society in online spaces. In this chapter, I shall demonstrate how Discourses of whiteness regulate and delimit what can be said or done in online spaces – which I call *discursive practices*, a term I adopt from Foucault (1978). In specific, I shall illustrate how discursive practices create a hierarchy among participants. Discourses of whiteness, as I have defined in the previous chapter, refer to the notion that whiteness itself has value for its possessor and grants sets of privileges (Delgado & Stefancic, 2012). In order to understand how Discourses of whiteness manifest themselves in practices, I analyse how discursive practices define the ways in which people navigate and learn in and through online learning contexts.

The nexus between discursive practices and identification constitutes how people understand each other, develop relationships, and act upon or react to one another (Yates & Hiles, 2010). If discursive practices dictate the identities that are accepted, legitimised, or included, and those that are othered or excluded, then discursive practices can never be equal or neutral. In other words, different individuals from different social categories experience discursive practices differently at any given time. This is what Crenshaw (1989) calls intersectionality. According to this perspective, dynamics of oppression operate differently for different individuals; thus, different identification categories (e.g., race, gender, class, sexual orientation, or nationality) should be examined in relation to each other since no person has a single identification (i.e. a person may be both gay and native-American or both female and black). An example can be found in a vignette Delgado and Stefancic (2012) provide about a hypothetical black woman who experiences workplace discrimination based on the combination of her race and gender. In this vignette, the woman's supervisor does not discriminate against black males or white females; thus, the discrimination she experiences cannot be explained just by race or gender but combination of both. It is only through considering these identification categories

58 Hierarchy of privilege

in combination with each other that we can explain how different individuals experience the world in different ways on different occasions.

I concur with these perspectives and employ intersectionality for understanding the nature of engagements in online spaces. Rather than asking how whites and non-whites experience online learning,[1] I seek to explain how identification and engagements are racialised with respect to privilege and diversity. By so doing, I seek to explain how discursive practices limit, shape, authorise, and legitimise the identifications that can be utilised and the meanings that they convey. With this approach, I hope to move beyond a mere description of who is who but illustrate how identification preserves power, privilege, and hierarchy with respect to race, ethnicity, and nationality. I underscore the fact that macro-level societal Discourses have a direct impact on how people identify themselves and others, and thus that such discourses affect subjectivities.

4.1 Discursive practices of identification

Discourses produce knowledge that provides a language for talking about a particular concept at a particular moment (Foucault, 1972). Multivalent and intertwined, discourses regulate the knowledge that is meaningful and the practices that are reasonable. In this sense, Discourses and societal power relations are inextricably related: Discourses produce differentiated power relations and these social relations in turn reproduce the very same Discourses. This circulation of production and reproduction of Discourses is what Foucault (1978) calls discursive practices. Discursive practices operate at every level of social life; therefore, they permeate all levels of social existence. There is no place outside of discursive systems (Hall, 2001). Discursive practices do not function in a linear form nor do they follow a single direction. They exist in a net-like formation; they are never monopolised by one centre. This suggests that each and every individual, to a certain extent, is caught up in this circulation of Discourses.

Discursive regimes have three characteristics: (1) they limit and define who can speak with what authority, (2) they limit and set the range of meanings available for individuals, and (3) they limit and impose specific roles on individuals (Foucault, 1978). In other words, they determine what one can think, say, and do in a given context. Online selves, then, are as much about what we imagine or feel about ourselves as they are about what we can think, say, or do. In what follows, I demonstrate how discursive practices of identification create racialised subjectivities that shape social engagements in online spaces. I will analyse how Discourses of whiteness create a hierarchy of privilege by which individuals are positioned in relation each other.

4.1.1 Privilege and power

Jeff is from Britain and identifies himself as a "white male, British in origin and from middle or lower-middle class". He calls himself an "economic migrant"

Hierarchy of privilege   59

as he has lived in different parts of the world as an English teacher: "I travelled where I can make income". This is his first online course and I asked him whether he was enjoying it:

> Um, . . . I think . . . I enjoy . . . not going to a classroom. And, it does allow anytime, anywhere access, but it has constraints. . . . Um, I thought it would be freer than it is. When you read articles about online learning, they sound like it is freer than it is. But it is still constrained. The only freedom is that I don't have to go to a class.

Curious about his definition of freedom, I asked him what he means by freer. Jeff was quick to talk about the democratising effects of online education:

> it has some sort of democratising effect for education because . . . um, if you have the Internet connection, then you get access to knowledge. People take this online knowledge, [take] this global knowledge and use it for their own local context. I believe it is a good example.

I reminded Jeff of the notion of the digital divide and asked him whether he believes online learning is "freer" with the divide in mind. He replied:

> Um, it is not if you think in that way. But it is not a productive way to think about. Yes, people in remote places may not have access yet, but it is a matter of time.

Following up his explanation, I asked him what he means by "people in remote places". Jeff explained that he meant "people in Africa . . . I don't know, maybe, some native tribes in somewhere". Jeff deftly racialised the notion of the digital divide by using racialised geographical locations.

Indeed, the digital divide is not only a geographical matter but also has a racial aspect. According to Warschauer and Matuchniak (2010), for example, while North America has higher Internet connection rates overall than other continents, whites have overwhelmingly higher and faster connection rates compared to blacks or browns. Jeff did not recognise this (saying "people in Africa" instead of "blacks") nor did he consider racial or ethnic dynamics in his explanation. Thus, he did not speak directly about racialised experiences in online education. Such avoidance was not exclusive to Jeff but was typical for white students overall when discussing issues such as access, online selves, or equity. White students' ignorance to racial discourses or their level of comfort with the assumption that they are exempt from discursive practices typify the notion that *white is not a race*, positioning as the norm by which others are positioned as racial beings. This can be explained through the concept of whiteness as normalisation or neutralisation; that is, social, political, and cultural advantages accorded to whites seem invisible to white people.

60 Hierarchy of privilege

According to Jeff's explanation, online education is supposed to be "free" or "more democratic" because people can "take global knowledge and use it for their local context". I asked Jeff whether he thinks that, according to his definition, online education is not a democratising tool but rather a means of colonisation since such knowledge represents white male perspectives of the Western world. Hesitant to give me a quick answer, he explained:

> Well, I meant it democratises to a certain extent. You know there is a great firewall of China.[2] There is a great amount of propaganda going on there because the type of knowledge they are getting is restricted. But it also . . . um, it still can change the society. The social media, in my experience in Singapore, has opened up people. It is difficult to police social media so people are bringing up all these social and political issues. So, it does have these effects in society, but it does not . . . um I am not super positive or sceptical about the effects of knowledge in such places. I think this is a lot better than the previous model. [. . .] I mean . . . I think the whole idea that knowledge is constructed, presented, and taken up is moving from the colonial model, rightly or wrongly. Colonial model is . . . it starts with the industrial revolution and enlightenment; it is a business model, Fordist model. I am not saying we are in a post-colonial era. English, or Anglo-Franco model of living still dominates the entire Internet, still; and the academia. . . . . Um, I think the Internet did and still does support or um, reinforce the colonial agenda but there is a much greater awareness of that right now and we are moving away from that era. But I agree with you to a certain extent. It might also reinforce status quo.

Analysing knowledge and the Internet with respect to colonial agendas, Jeff was able to consider that online education – or the Internet in general – may not be as democratic as he first suggested. By acknowledging that "Anglo-Franco model of living" "might reinforce status quo" in online interactions, Jeff recognised that Discourses of whiteness may affect how one experiences online learning, albeit tangentially.

The conversation returned to Jeff's online learning experience. I asked him what he thinks of the relationship between his race, gender, and class and his status quo. He replied right away: "It is my privilege. It is the positive discrimination I experience". We had the following exchange:

MURAT: Positive discrimination?
JEFF: It is difficult to . . . um, . . . Well, most of the discrimination I experience is positive. You know . . . they look at my name, they look at my picture, they probably look at my nationality. There are a lot of positive things about it in online context. What I mean is that there are a lot of positive connotations that go along with my name and gender and . . . my nationality and my . . . race. But, uh, I don't want to say that I am all being spoiled or something like that (laughs). But also, there are certain expectations.

Hierarchy of privilege 61

MURAT: Like?

JEFF: To be intelligent, I suppose. To be able to write clearly and concisely. Maybe I give myself these expectations, I don't know but you know what I mean? There is always this . . . belief um, . . . this understanding that . . . that I have to be as such, right?

Jeff suggested that the positive discrimination he experiences was based on his name and his picture in his profile page. He suggested that his identification carries positive discrimination. According to him, being White connoted the impression that he was – and perhaps other Whites were – intelligent and deserving. I was intrigued by his suggestion that he has to be as such, and asked:

MURAT: What do you mean?

JEFF: I mean . . . my positive discrimination is . . ., um . . . cultural, if you like. It is something I am privileged to have; just because of the world we live in. It is given to me just because the culture I am coming from. Not that I like it or want it or . . . I, um, . . . I didn't ask for it. But the positive discrimination is that you have to have privileged . . . um, be privileged on minorities.

MURAT: How about negative discrimination?

JEFF: Oh, there is. . . . Um, actually, . . . you know, I don't know. . . . I don't know enough about it; I never experienced it but I imagine there must be. You know dominant social structures exist everywhere and I am sure that dominant power structures exist online. So, people, um, want to hold on to those power structures in online courses, too. But it is not necessarily a gender or ethnic thing, it is simply, purely about power. I experienced those dominant power relations from my privileged background. So, those power relations exist anywhere in any context. It is not simply White male domination. (laughs). What about a White female, right? So, I don't know anything about negative discrimination. I don't know.

Jeff defined one way in which Discourses of whiteness operate in online courses. He thought he is privileged to experience positive discrimination simply because he is identified as white. In other words, he believed that he does not have to do anything to deserve his privilege: "It is given to me just because the culture I am coming from". This is what Harris (1993) calls whiteness as a form of property: whiteness has a value in itself. In particular, Discourses of whiteness provide a symbolic privilege that conceptions of beauty or intelligence not only are tied to whiteness but also necessarily exclude those who are identified as non-white. This was evident in Jeff's explanation as he suggested that he is privileged over minorities.

Jeff considered power separate from race, ethnicity, or gender; therefore, he claimed that his discrimination was not "a gender or ethnic thing [but] it is simply, purely about power". However, Discourses should be addressed within power relations in order to understand how they normalise and justify

62 Hierarchy of privilege

discrimination against those who fall outside the idealisations of such discourses (Giroux, 2011). In the passage above, by separating ethnicity from power, Jeff cannot comprehend whiteness as a social structure that systematically oppresses those who are identified as non-white. The accounts Jeff provided reflect ideas core to the purpose of the present chapter. When Jeff articulated his online learning experience with regards to race, ethnicity, gender, and class, he was able to talk about his online learning experience in terms of privilege, discrimination, and power. For Jeff, and for many students I interviewed, intelligence, privilege, and positive discrimination are given to those that are identified as white. Being entitled to positive discrimination and privilege was equated with being white; thus, power and status quo was racialised in the online courses I examined. The direct consequence of this is that whites and non-whites are positioned in relation to each other.

Kate, whose family origin goes back to England, Scotland, and Ireland, identified herself as white. She is a teacher at one of the neighbouring city's school boards and she constantly made connections to her profession as we talked. She described herself as "not only an experienced teacher but also an experienced online student since this is [her] tenth online course". She resides three hours' drive away from the campus and she travels to the main campus "only once at the beginning of each semester, just to smell the air and get the feeling of being a student". Since she is physically away from the campus, I asked her opinion about the statement that online education allows anytime-anywhere access. She answered that "it provides great benefits" but she continues "there are some equity issues regarding the access . . . um, to tools, to equipment, or to the Internet". Kate brought up the issue of equity even before I mentioned or asked about it. However, Kate addressed equity in terms of access to the Internet and thus she echoed the popular notion of a digital gap or digital divide[3] without acknowledging the racial aspects of it. Likewise, she neglected race and ethnicity as important aspects of equity. Kate's focus on the digital divide – despite its direct relation to social class – allowed her to talk about equity without questioning her privilege or status quo.

I asked her whether she thinks that there would no longer be any issues of equity or social justice if everybody had access to the Internet:

KATE: I think, um . . . I think if everybody would have had access to the Internet, I think . . . I think there would be fewer issues of equity. Like . . . um. . . . If we all had equal opportunity to participate, there would be fewer issues of equity.

MURAT: What issues would there be?

KATE: Um, maybe . . . some people would be anxious to participate because they never participated online before. You know. . . . This is something new for many people, so there, um . . . so, it might be stressful for some people.

I was curious why Kate thinks this is an issue of equity. I asked:

Hierarchy of privilege 63

MURAT: So, what does it mean for participation?

KATE: Well, people would participate less, right? So, it is all about participation.

Kate used the concepts of equity and equality interchangeably. As I have argued in Chapter 2, equity refers to qualitative judgements of whether a given situation is just or fair. Yet, the way Kate used the term suggests that she meant sameness in quantity of participation; that is, equality. I asked her to consider opportunities to participate in relation to her ethnicity. Puzzled, she said:

> I am a teacher, so, when . . . um, so, I always see how that privilege works in schools. When we talk about privilege in schools, we always consider students' background; background in terms of race and ethnicity, and, um, in terms of socio-economic background. I come from a privileged background. I am third generation Canadian and my family background is going back to England, Scotland, and Ireland. So, . . . I come from a background, where [. . .] I am privileged. I have access to technology . . . um, to the Internet and I am pursuing my master's degree, which is a privilege by itself because . . . because it is higher education and even beyond higher education. So, yeah, I do experience that privilege.

Kate now acknowledged that she believes she is privileged because of her ethnicity and recognised that her privilege allowed her to pursue her academic degree online. Thus, Kate linked her academic achievements with her privilege. Curious about how she understands the role of her privilege in the online learning space, I asked Kate how she utilises her privilege.

KATE: I think it is important for me to bring up my privilege because the whole notion of digital gap is related to privilege; so I believe it is important for me to stress that . . . that aspect of my background.

MURAT: How did you experience that privilege?

KATE: I would like to think that my privilege does not matter, I would like to think it doesn't have anything to do with it but it does; unfortunately it does. You know . . . just my name itself can tell a lot about myself, and my background, perhaps. And also my picture and name can say a lot about myself; it says a lot about my privileged background. I mean, I wish there . . . I wish my privilege was not in play but it is in play. It is inevitable.

MURAT: What does it mean to be privileged in online learning?

KATE: Well, it means that you know more. . . . Um, for example, the person I am currently working with for this final project is not Canadian. And she is not Caucasian either. Um, . . . um, and we work on things that . . . um, well, when we work on the final paper together, I can say that I have certain advantages over her but I try not to over-power her. Only because she is not Canadian, I can tell that I am more knowledgeable about the subject matter because we deal with Canadian stuff. I mean . . . I mean, the context is in Canada and we deal with Canadian schools and Canadian

64 Hierarchy of privilege

> school system, so I know more than her, more than non-Caucasians. Um, I guess, it is mostly because of the context. So I am privileged not because of my ethnicity but also because of the context. So, um, I am privileged . . . um, through my ethnicity in relation to the context.

For Kate, her privilege – that she is identified as white/Caucasian – meant that she knows more about the subject matter. Thus, Kate affirmed the notion that intelligence is a property of whiteness and that being identified as white has an intrinsic value. Another important point is that Kate not only suggested that being identified as Canadian is a form of privilege but also equates being Canadian with being white. By so doing, Kate reflects Bannerji (2000)'s notion of *hyphened-Canadians*; that is, whites are accepted as default Canadians and non-whites are identified with their hyphened ethnicity or nationality. Consequently, Kate's explanation of her privilege reflects the colonial and white-supremacist Discourses in which the educational institution of this research is grounded.

What both Kate and Jeff suggested is that being identified as white carries privilege and that those who are identified as non-white or non-Canadian are perhaps less knowledgeable unless otherwise demonstrated by personal characteristics, professional experience, or academic success. This was particularly true for Gulsum, who identifies herself as non-white. She was born in Egypt and immigrated to Canada with her husband and three children almost ten years ago. I asked Gulsum whether she considered herself as white before she immigrated to Canada.[4] She answered:

> Um, not really. I am not sure actually. (laughs). I never thought about it before I came here. I mean we had tourists and foreigners and they were white but in Egypt, we don't talk about it. We all are the same there, so we don't need such . . . um, racial understanding to . . . separate people. I mean . . . I mean, maybe we all are accepted as white or not; I don't know but it didn't matter because we never think of us in that way.

Gulsum's explanation that she didn't think of her race or ethnicity before she came to Canada hinted that she is now more aware of such issues. I asked her whether she makes sense of her ethnicity now and she responded by nodding. I asked Gulsum how she makes sense of her racial identification in the online course. She said that she believes she has to "prove [herself] as a successful student, who knows as much as [her] peers". Gulsum echoed what Jeff and Kate suggested in the excerpts above and racialised intelligence and success. As identified non-white, Gulsum believed that she is not accepted as intelligent or as successful; thus, she had to create the impression that she is as intelligent and as successful as those identified as white. She continued:

> I always underscore my achievements um, . . . because when people look at me or um, talk to me, I want them to know that I know things . . . um,

know things as much as they do. So, like, . . . I want to put forward my achievements but not limited with my academic life but also, I put forward my achievements in my professional life. I am a non-white, Muslim-Canadian so I want my achievements . . . to overshadow any prejudice um, . . . any judgement that whites make.

I was interested in understanding why she does not identify herself as white. I reminded Gulsum that according to the Canadian census, people from the Middle East and North Africa are accepted as White. She replied to me right away: "Well, I am not white enough . . . you know what I mean?". By saying that she is not white enough, Gulsum reiterated the notion that whiteness is not about phenotype or geographical location but is a social, political, and historical construction. I was curious about how she experiences online learning with respect to her racial and ethnic identification:

MURAT: What does that mean for your online learning experience?
GULSUM: People know that I am not from here; I am not Canadian enough for them.

Gulsum was aware of the colonial and white-supremacist Discourses, and echoed Kate (and indeed the notion of *hyphened-Canadian*) when she suggested that she is not Canadian enough simply because she is not white enough. Gulsum added:

So, they think that I am . . . um, they think I don't know things. So I am trying to show my intelligence so that I can break their bias against me. I am trying to show that I can be intelligent even though I am not white. Or, partially white. (laughs).

She continued and brought a new aspect to the fore:

GULSUM: You know that bias, right? You are not Canadian either so you must have experienced that, too.
MURAT: What bias?
GULSUM: That Muslims are fools, in a sense. Whites think that we are not intelligent because I am covered. That is . . . bias against Muslims.[5]

Gulsum pointed out how Discourses of whiteness are manifest in Discourses about religion and how Islamophobia can be a form of racialised identification. She believed that if she was "British or Scottish", people would not consider her "as a deficit person". I wondered how she experiences Islamophobia in online learning:

MURAT: Do you think this is somehow related to your race or ethnicity?

66 Hierarchy of privilege

GULSUM: Um, it must be. I mean . . . if . . . I were white enough or [if I were] British or Scottish, people wouldn't ask me . . . um, they wouldn't consider me as a deficit person.
MURAT: Deficit?
GULSUM: You know . . . as . . . um . . . as less intelligent.

After this conversation Gulsum and I exchanged our thoughts and beliefs regarding Islamophobia. Even though I explained to Gulsum that I do not associate myself with any religion or belief system, we exchanged many stories regarding religious biases and discrimination. I asked Gulsum what all of these mean for her learning. She said:

> I try to participate. I show how intelligent I am. If they don't see it, I can't do anything about it, right? So, if um, if they don't see it, then it is their . . . loss. You know what, I tried but I don't care anymore. I am in Canada for more than ten years and after all that racial discrimination I faced, this . . . online, um, what happens [in] online courses don't hurt me anymore. I am immune now; [. . .] immune from all racism and discrimination.

Gulsum's words were striking. She believed she was and still has been discriminated based on her ethnicity and religion; that is, she is identified as non-white and thus believed to be inferior to those identified as white. This inferiority paradigm is built on the belief that non-whites are biologically or genetically less intelligent than whites, a notion that is based on IQ studies (Tate, 1997). Gulsum suggested that the inferiority paradigm is manifest in her online learning experience. Such experience, however, shows striking contrasts to Devran's.[6]

Devran is an international student from Turkey. Devran identifies herself as White, Turkish, female, and from the lower-middle class. She suggested that she was able to "openly and freely participate because [she] was able to log in and join the discussion anytime [she] wanted". I invited her to consider her participation in relation to her race or ethnicity and I asked her whether she sensed or experienced any sort of privilege. Devran rejected such privilege right away; however, she added:

> um . . . I, um, . . . in fact, I sort of think that some people were more privileged, and some people were under-privileged. But not me; at least I don't think so. I mean, I . . . would . . . realise that I was privileged if I really were; but again, I felt I was . . . um, sort of in a balance. I was not privileged . . . but also not under-privileged.

Devran's hesitation was typical among those who consider open and free participation simply in terms of access to the online space. When I challenged the issue of access and suggested she consider participation and identification in terms of race and ethnicity, Devran – and almost all of the participants – acknowledged participation as a discursive practice:

MURAT: Who, then, is privileged and under-privileged?
DEVRAN: Um . . . those who are . . . who come from or have British origin. They are privileged. And those under-privileged ones are . . . those who are. . . . Um, under-privileged ones are all the others.
MURAT: How about you? You suggest that you are neither privileged or under-privileged. How is that possible?
DEVRAN: Well, I am not under-privileged because I am white but at the same time I am not privileged because I am not British in origin.

Although it was evident in Devran's explanation that she believed privilege – or under-privilege – is a matter of ethnicity, she insisted on not defining privilege in terms of ethnicity until I directly asked her:

MURAT: What's the difference between being British in origin and being Turkish in origin?
DEVRAN: Um, I guess the difference is something to do with Canada's history, right? Anyone from British origin, or French origin is . . . Like, I mean, if you are from Turkey, you are not from the first colonisers, so you are not privileged but you are not black or Asian, so you are still white.
MURAT: So, do you mean privilege is a matter of ethnicity with respect to colonisation?
DEVRAN: Yes! Exactly what I am trying to say. Thanks (laughs).

By racialising their identification, both Devran and Gulsum understood their online learning experience as a discursive process. They both suggested that they are "not that white". However, while Gulsum believed she was racially discriminated against, Devran put herself into a more balanced position as she believed she was neither privileged nor under-privileged. In this sense, Devran suggested an ethnic or racial hierarchy that classifies individuals from most privileged to under-privileged: those who are identified as white are on the top, those who are identified as non-Canadian whites are in the middle, and all the rest are at the bottom of the hierarchy of privilege.

Johanne offered another possible hierarchy of privilege. She identifies herself as Caribbean-Canadian: "I was born in a Caribbean country, but we moved here when I was two years old. So, I grew up in Canada; therefore, I am Caribbean-Canadian". I asked her what it means to be a Caribbean-Canadian in an online course; she replied without any hesitation: "it means you are more of a Caribbean than a Canadian". For Johanne, the online course was "a White place, anyway" and she did "not want to have any conflict" about her identification since she was not sure whether she is entitled to be "accepted as Canadian anyway". Similar to everyone else I interviewed, Johanne suggested the

68 Hierarchy of privilege

implicit understanding that whites are real Canadians and others are somehow peripheral Canadians. In other words, along with all my participants, Johanne illustrated the colonial and white-supremacist understanding of Canada as an imagined nation of whites:

> I usually speak about my Caribbean background more so than my Canadian background because I don't think I would be defined, um, . . . or accepted as a Canadian. If you look at me in online [courses], people think of me as Caribbean, as immigrant or minority. But you know what, if I was white, I would be defined as Canadian automatically. So, I am speaking from my Caribbean background because I don't want to have any conflict, right. Besides, it is a white place anyway; you don't need to speak from white perspective because everything or everyone is already white.

Arguing that "it is a White place" and "everyone is already White", Johanne pointed out to the fact that Discourses of whiteness are accepted as normative and neutral standards, against which all non-Whites are measured or judged. Therefore, she suggested that Discourses of whiteness were manifest in the online learning space and that they determine how individuals can be identified.

I asked Johanne what she meant when she said that she speaks from her Caribbean background because she did not want to have any conflict. I was interested in how this conflict affects her participation. She was quick to talk about power and privilege:

> I believe, um, it is about . . . sort of privilege or power let's say. You know what I mean? When you are not coming from white, um, or let's say from non-English background, you are put in a . . . less-valued or less-privileged category. And this is not only for me, but it is also so for people from Eastern-Europe, like Polish or Bulgarian people. You are not Canadian no matter what. Right? And, you are put into this . . . um, minority category. But it is true though; there are some privileged groups and you either belong to it or um, or . . . out of it.

Johanne's explanation of identification shifted from a sole racial understanding (that all white-Canadians are real Canadians) to a colonial understanding (that only whites and Anglo-in-origin are real Canadians). According to her, privilege was a matter of ethnicity along with national background (one still has to be white and English at the same time) and one is either entitled to privilege or not, based on such criteria.

For individuals I interviewed, race, ethnicity, and national origin defined the hierarchy of privilege. Though those who are identified as white acknowledged their privilege and indeed placed themselves on top of the hierarchy, they cannot categorise how others were positioned in such a hierarchy. That

Hierarchy of privilege 69

is, for many whites, they were on top of the hierarchy and "non-whites and all the others and immigrants" – as Denise puts it – were somehow positioned below.

The hierarchy of privilege and the positions individuals occupy in this hierarchy, then, define the discursive practices around identification. Such discursive practices around identification determine who can be identified as white or Canadian in order to be entitled to symbolic privilege, stemming from the Discourses of whiteness. Discursive practices, therefore, enforce an implicit understanding that individuals must somehow position themselves in this hierarchy of privilege. This implicit understanding determines the rules by which people engage with each other in online discussions. For example, those who are identified as non-white have to convey the impression that they are as successful, as intelligent, and as good as their white counterparts. In other words, those who are identified as non-white have to be "white enough" to be accepted as intelligent.

4.1.2 Diversity vs. hierarchy

As discussed in Chapter 2, online education research takes sense of community as a given, focusing only on the positive aspects while disregarding the discursive practices that might be problematic. The notion of diversity is often used to explain the benefits of group work: that it gives students opportunities to talk to, share with, and learn from each other. However, when not carefully planned and cautiously applied, group work may exacerbate unfairness among group members. Diversity, then, is central in my analysis for exploring how hierarchy of privilege is understood and utilised.

Sydney is a white female and her "family origin goes back to England". She is a "second generation Canadian" and she works as a part-time teacher at the city's school board. She "really enjoys [her] online course because [she] loves interacting with different people":

> It is very diverse, the [online] course, I mean. We all are different. We have different racial and ethnic backgrounds; we have different identities. I am white and Canadian, someone else is white but not Canadian, someone else is not white but Canadian. It is all different. And it is not limited with . . . just with race or ethnicity. Um, like, for example, I am a part-time teacher and someone else might be a full-time teacher, teaching same or different topics or grade levels. I live in Canada but someone else might be living in who knows where, right? Or . . . or, like I travel. I travelled to Africa and been there and someone else might be travelled to . . . let's say South America.

With reference to race and ethnicity, Sydney's definition of diversity was initially racialised. However, she quickly moved from the definition of diversity

70 Hierarchy of privilege

as a trait of certain cultural groups to diversity as stories of certain individuals. I was interested in understanding what constitutes diversity for Sydney. She said:

> There is always something that makes us someone different . . . we all are diverse in a sense. We all are from different parts of the world. Right? This person is from Asia, this one from Caribbean, another one is from Turkey; all over the world.

For Sydney, individuals from different parts of the World make the online course diverse. Thus, she considered diversity as traits of individuals. I wondered what Sydney thinks of the role diversity plays in online learning. She answered:

> it adds up to the conversation. It makes the discussion richer and, um, it makes it more sound. It is . . . I like that diversity because . . . we . . . then, have different opinions and . . . um, we will be able to add something to discussion.

Sydney – and other students identified as white – tended to address diversity as a commodity of those individuals identified as non-white. This approach to diversity typifies the notion that whites are accepted as the norm. This was also true for Denise, who identifies herself as Anglo-white, and who suggested that "the group is diverse because [they] all come from different places and [they] all have different interests". Amy, who is white and of Irish descent, similarly believed that "the online course is such a diverse place because people [in online courses] are from all around the world".

When diversity is accepted as an individual characteristic rather than a group trait, students identified as white can avoid the social, political, economic, and historical aspects of diversity (Gaztambide-Fernández, 2009). In particular, talking about diversity as personal difference allowed students – particularly those who identify themselves as white – to disregard discursive practices that preserve their status quo within such diverse groups. That is, by addressing diversity as "different perspectives that different people bring to discussion", as Courtney puts it, white students saw themselves as the norm while seeing others as those who can "enrich" the discussion and "diversify" their learning context. Non-white students, then, were identified as those who are different and thus who were supposed to provide diverse perspectives.

Johanne, "Caribbean-Canadian", also believes that the online learning space is a diverse place. She defines diversity as involving characteristics of racial and ethnic groups, but she seems puzzled, and her typically smiling face is etched with confusion:

> The course is very diverse. And when I say diverse, I mean different racial and ethnic backgrounds. [. . .] And sometimes such different ethnicities

come into play in discussions. And, um, . . . there is . . . a common courtesy that . . . you have to acknowledge your peer's idea but suggest yours (perspective) too. Like, um, . . . for example, "I understand your idea, but how about considering this idea because I am coming from this background and perspective". [. . .] Otherwise, this is harsh, right? You have to remember that you are talking to a human; there is a human on the other side. You have to remember that everyone is coming from a different background; everyone has different identity, different culture. So, what I am saying is not totally wrong; it is just . . . that . . . there are other perspectives, too; and I want them to consider my perspective, too. But it all goes back to dominant ideology, right? How would you know there are other perspectives if you are coming from dominant ideology? Right? But there are. We all are different.

Because Johanne addresses "diversity" with respect to racial and ethnic identification, she was able to talk about the effects of Discourses on "diverse" groups. According to her, there was a tension between diversity and Discourses of whiteness; that is, her perspectives were not considered nor acknowledged. Johanne's final comments about dominant ideology[7] points out what is known as white ignorance, a notion that Discourses of whiteness are invisible for those identified as white since such Discourses are accepted as normative and neutral (Mills, 1998). I asked her to explain what she meant by ideology, particularly dominant ideology:

JOHANNE: It is . . . um, it is this general belief about things. It is like . . . knowing something without knowing how you know it. I guess what I am trying to say is that it is a narrative that, um, . . . defines the things or people or meanings . . . in a way they are. And there is not only one narrative but um, there are many narratives that . . . are infused in society. And, it is infused in online learning environments, too.

MURAT: How does it manifest itself in online learning?

JOHANNE: It is because many students are coming from dominant ideology. Um, you know what, I am not sure. I mean, um, . . . I mean it is kind of like . . . because that society has many dominant ideologies . . . and . . . that ideology is infused in everything. So, ideology is manifest in . . . in . . . um, in all of us. So, it is likely that dominant ideology will be picked up in online learning too. I guess my answer is that people just assert their position and um, . . . exercise that position; and they bring that dominant ideology.

MURAT: And, what is this dominant ideology in online learning?

JOHANNE: Oh, it is whiteness. It categorises us; it under-privileges us. [. . .] It is simply the hidden curriculum. It happens when one view is seen as the norm. And, when there are other people over there in the mediated space, they might want to bring in their identity. Like, I mean . . ., you know . . . there are different identities; different races, different gender,

72   Hierarchy of privilege

ethnicity, sexual orientation, and so on and so forth. People want to bring in these in their online experiences. Um, . . . so, in some cases, these identities may clash with dominant ideology. So, I am not sure if it is fair for people like us.

Despite being not sure, Johanne defined ideology in terms of identification. She posited that ideology is something that defines meanings, roles, and enactments; thus, she suggested that it is implicit in the online curriculum. Interested in diversity, I asked:

MURAT: What do you think all these mean for diversity? How does ideology work out in the community?
JOHANNE: Well, I believe that diversity is just a term to cover this racism. Um, maybe I should not call it racism. But anyway, it is a way to cover what is really happening online. Um, for example, diversity is taken like "oh, let's learn about your food" or "let's learn about your music". It is always superficial; it is always taken as something good. But on the other hand, you need that community; and without it, you have no learning. So, it is interesting, isn't it?
MURAT: So, what does that mean for you?
JOHANNE: Well, um . . . It means that, um, it means that I am different and it means that it is not easy to be different or diverse. So, again, I am not sure if it is fair.

Johanne thought of diversity as cultural traits; therefore, she was able to address diversity in relation to discursive practices – something that white students cannot acknowledge or recognise. By bringing discursive practices into her analysis, she questioned diversity and the hierarchy of privilege with respect to equity or, in her words, fairness.[8]

Nalini is a "second generation Canadian", who identifies herself as "Indian-Canadian even though [she] was born and grew up in Canada". She believed that her online interactions were "rich" because "the [online] course has diverse people from all over the world". "It is a multicultural learning platform", she said. Indeed, Nalini echoed the multicultural discourse – and her white peers – that people bring diversity and that somehow everyone learns from each other. I asked her to elaborate more on what she means by rich interactions:

NALINI: Rich, like different things . . . like, um, for example, diversity in experiences or perspectives. . . . Um, maybe like different ethnicities. Things like that.
MURAT: So, how do you bring these different experiences or perspectives?
NALINI: Um, like . . . I bring in my perspective when I discuss with someone. So, in a sense, I bring that richness. (laughs). I enrich the discussion with my difference, with perspectives.

MURAT: But you said you were born and grew up in Canada. What kind of difference do you think you bring in?

NALINI: Um, right . . . Um, I believe that . . . that I am more Indian than Canadian online; perhaps . . . because I am sort of um, . . . taken as Indian. I never realised that I was that Indian but I am. So, I bring in that culture with me; bring that Indian culture with me and add my experiences and perspectives.

Despite how Nalini self-identifies as Indian–Canadian, she says that her peers identify her as Indian; thus, she believes that she brings diversity and enriches discussions by enacting Indian:

> I enrich discussions because I bring in that different culture people need. You know, you need different perspectives to learn from others. So, I do that. I feel like I am more Indian and um, . . . that diversity has a lot to do with learning. And, um I am Indian . . . and . . . someone else represents some other culture and this is how we diversify learning experience.

Nalini saw herself as someone from whom others can learn. Nalini's definition of herself can be explained as being the curriculum of diversity. Gaztambide-Fernández (2009) uses *the curriculum of diversity* to illustrate how those who are identified as non-white have to negotiate their status as an element of diversity. Nalini's accounts suggest the same is true in online learning spaces. Nalini believed it is her role to enrich and diversify online learning. I was curious whether Nalini had a chance to benefit from the diversity in the online course. I asked her if she has learned anything from someone who is different from her:

NALINI: There are always blacks, and Asians, and . . . Latinos. I don't know. . . . There are people from Middle East. What I am saying is that there are always different people that you can learn from.

MURAT: How come you didn't mention whites or Indigenous people, like anyone from First Nations? Didn't you learn anything from them?

NALINI: (laughs). Nah. What can you learn from whites? You already know it. And as for Indigenous people, they are not there. So how can I learn from them, right?

Both Nalini and Johanne identified themselves as Canadians. However, their status in the hierarchy of privilege positioned them as being different. In return, they believed that they were there to enrich online discussion. Hierarchy of privilege, then, positions those who are identified as white at the centre while others are positioned as different. Therefore, for both Nalini and Johanne, diversity meant that they are different and that they were supposed to bring their differences to enrich discussions.

74 Hierarchy of privilege

Despite the fact that Devran identifies herself as white – but not necessarily with British origin – she believed she was "somehow different" and she should "bring [her] difference into discussions". She said she was "white but still different, maybe because [she] do[es] not represent the mainstream whiteness". I asked her to explain what she meant:

> You know . . . if you are Turkish, you are still white but . . . you are not white as someone like Canadian or American or English. It is like, um, different um, . . . different whiteness. I am not sure how to explain this but . . . I guess one thing I can say is that I am different in a way that I am from Turkey.

Devran's commentary suggested that she was not privileged enough to claim herself as white; thus, she was positioned as "somehow" different. Indeed, Devran's explanation pointed out the fact that whiteness was not a biological category but a social construction. Consequently, who can be identified as white was a social construction and thus it can change based on what is at stake (for example, in the early 20th century, Italians, Irish, or Jews were not identified as white in the United States). Though Devran counted as white according to Canadian census, she was not identified as white in a context shaped by social, political, and historical dynamics.

For Gulsum, "diversity has a lot to do with assimilation". She believed she has "to conform to the dominant culture and assimilate herself; otherwise [she has to] face the consequences, like alienation or discrimination". According to her, "diversity has nothing to do with whites". I was puzzled by this statement:

MURAT: What do you mean by that?
GULSUM: I mean, they have nothing to lose. Diversity is not about them, it is about us; it is about us . . . giving up from ourselves but accepting what they want us to be. It has nothing to do with whites because they are . . . in a sense . . . mainstream.
MURAT: So, when you say "diversity has nothing to do with whites", do you mean they are the norm?
GULSUM: Exactly!

Gulsum echoed Devran, Nalini, and Johanne that students who are identified as white constitute the norm and that others are somehow different, and that it is the "others" who have to position themselves somewhere in the hierarchy of privilege.

These accounts and insights suggest that discursive practices define who can claim certain roles and privileges. Hierarchy of privilege, then, positions white-Canadians as the norm and all the others as somehow different. Those who are identified as different have to understand what makes them different and

Hierarchy of privilege   75

enact their differences by enriching curriculum and diversifying learning experiences. Consequently, rather than echoing the optimistic and idealistic understanding in the literature of online education supporting a diversity from which all students benefit, it appears that those who are identified as non-white are themselves the diversity from which those who are identified as white can learn.

4.2 Negotiation of difference and diversity

So far, I have demonstrated that discursive practices of identification position individuals within a hierarchy of privilege. Nevertheless, it is possible for individuals to resist or struggle against such discursive positioning – and against power structures that reproduce such Discourses (Foucault, 1978). Temporary inversions of power relations enable individuals to negotiate their identification and redefine their positions available to them.[9] Indeed, individuals who were identified as different or other did not seem to occupy their position in an unproblematic fashion.

Devran believed that she was able to challenge her position within the hierarchy of privilege:

> I was actually able to challenge that understanding. I was able to challenge people, especially those who think that I am um, . . . sort of a person . . . um, who thinks that I am less privileged, let's say. So, I was able to speak up for myself. I did it.

Devran was able to speak up for herself; however, she was not sure whether she was accepted as a legitimate participant. She continued:

> But it doesn't matter if they still don't see me as a real participant. It is ok. And it is ok only because I needed to . . . and was able to challenge that. And it is enough for me.

I asked Devran why she felt that she needed to challenge her peers.

DEVRAN: I think if you. . . . So, for example, if you are living in Canada or someone lives in India and other person lives in Turkey, they all are coming from totally different cultures. So, let's say that the course is being offered in Canada. Um, it may just have . . . um, let's just say [the online course] has dominant culture that complements Canadian understanding. And if you are coming from India, Turkey, or let's say Mexico, you are kind of in this space, um, where Canadian ideology is in everywhere. So you have to acknowledge or accept this Canadian perspective. And, I think most of the time it is not intentional. I think sometimes it is unintentional. Only because this is the culture we are embedded in. But you don't only accept

76 Hierarchy of privilege

the ideology but also challenge it. You need to challenge this Canadian ideology but also you need to challenge your own identity, too.

MURAT: What do you mean by that? How do you challenge Canadian ideology or your own identity?

DEVRAN: Um, it is just saying out loud that . . . saying that you are not who they think you are.

MURAT: And how is it related to Canadian ideology?

DEVRAN: Oh, it is just um, that . . . they are Canadian and I am Turkish so there is this understanding that I have to be, I guess, a certain person. You know. . . . Like, I am being stereotyped. But I can face that. It is ok. I am very vocal, and I can say right away if people are wrong about me.

Although Devran posited that she was able to speak up for herself and challenge her discursive position within the hierarchy of privilege, Nalini was not able to stand up for herself. Nalini articulated that she did not take any action regarding her identification as other because she was afraid of being excluded from discussions. She said:

I told you I was [accepted as] more Indian than Canadian, right? So, I was playing um, . . . um, not playing; it is somewhat harsh to say. But let's say I was bringing up more of my Indian perspectives because . . . simply you accept the dominant ideology and represent yourself to go along with it. Because, um. . . . You need to get accepted, you need to fit in if you want to participate. You don't want to be left out. You want to fit in.

Nalini's fear of isolation suggests that she does not have the power to challenge her discursive position.

For Sofia, who identifies herself as Latina, challenging the discursive positioning is a balancing act between anonymity and identification. She believed that there is always a decision that she had to make about her position within the hierarchy:

it is always a decision about how much you can bring in your experience. Um, . . . um, it is a matter of how much you use your identity or um . . ., perspectives. It is about how much you reveal yourself. But, you have to use your identities because this is where you come from; this is why you think in a way that you think. So, it is always a tension that whether you can bring your perspectives or not; always a question whether you reveal yourself or stay anonymous and pretend that you agree with others. It is always about cultural identity.

Sofia is a permanent resident who came to Canada almost six years ago as a student. She believed that she is not that different; "in fact, [she is] just a normal person, like anyone else". However, she said that she plays her otherness and difference because she did not want to "have any conflict over cultural beliefs, which might lead to disconnection or isolation". I asked her why she plays her otherness rather than trying to be who she wants to be. She said:

> it is not that simple, you know. You are already defined, um, your role is already defined for you and you . . . you either play it and get along with people or just don't play it and face the consequences. You have to accommodate your role and yourself; you have to find a balance there; otherwise you have no learning. I guess, . . . I guess, I play that [Latina] identity in my regular life, so, why not online? So, I just don't care much anymore.

Sofia's explanation paralleled Nalini's fear of isolation. They both suggested that they have to play their "difference", otherwise they believed that they may be excluded from discussions. By playing their difference, Sofia and Nalini find ways in which they can participate. These accounts can illustrate how Discourses of whiteness not only delimit identifications available for individuals but also determine the ways in which one can participate in discussions.

Gulsum echoed both Sofia and Nalini, and posited that her identification is already determined for her:

GULSUM: I think it is because . . . sometimes they assume that because, um, because you are coming from a certain culture or coming from a different culture so to say. . . . So, they think you must be different, or you must be that certain people that they think for you.
MURAT: So, how come you don't tell them who you really are?
GULSUM: It is about fitting into dominant discourse. Absolutely! Nobody wants to be judged or nobody wants to be left out. So, you want to be included; you want to be part of the culture, part of the community. It is also an issue of control; control in terms of your image and your [online] self.

Sofia, Nalini, and Gulsum accepted that Discourses of whiteness delimit and determine their positions in their learning community. However, as I shall demonstrate in the next chapter, they play with their social presence and social absence as they make strategic choices and navigate the racial terrain of online learning space.

Johanne was "ready for struggle even though it is not easy", she said. I was curious about what it meant for her to challenge her identification or position within her online community. She explained that it is a constant struggle:

> Um, I . . . um, . . . how I deal with that is . . . um, honestly, it is not easy. I mean you can do it, but you constantly challenge people and struggle with them . . ., um, struggle about your perspectives. I do necessarily stress that I am Canadian too so that I can make sense but . . . it is hard, you know. Just because you are white, it doesn't make you more Canadian. But

78 Hierarchy of privilege

it makes them right to begin with. You know what I mean. Just because they are white and whiteness is the dominant ideology, they are right. And then, you fit in; and then, you can try to prove them otherwise. [. . .] but you have to do that. And sometimes it is frustrating, but you have to bring that up.

I asked her what the reaction was when she speaks up for herself:

JOHANNE: When you do that, people get caught off guard. They get really caught off guard because they don't expect you to say something about it. It is not easy but at the same time, you have to do that. They don't like it. They really don't like it. And you feel that they will come back at you at some point in the future because you challenge their dominant ideology, but this is what it is. I am not being rude. I am standing up for myself. You cannot do it all the time; you still have to know when to do it. But you have to. Otherwise I cannot learn. People, um, . . . let me say that, um, white people do not realise they can be mean and they can hurt you with jokes because they do not realise it. But it is all about race and ethnicity.

MURAT: How come?

JOHANNE: Whiteness is manifest subtly. Nobody is doing it bluntly or overtly. It is subtle and embedded, you know. I think, . . . um, I can. . . . Um, it is ironic because when I identify myself as Canadian, people are like "well, you are not really Canadian anyway, aren't you?" (laughs). In certain discussions, people want to ask you that; you can feel it. They want to ask you whether you are, um, or can be Canadian. So, I have to position myself before I put a note there. I have to clarify. And those people . . . um, they are cautious, right? They don't want to be labelled as racist. Otherwise it is a social suicide, right? So, being online is always about adjusting yourself accordingly . . . um, according to the dominant ideology. It is still there, right? So, you can't go against it but sometimes you cannot accept it either. So, you have to be careful and position yourself carefully. It is a balance in a way. And to be honest, it is very hard sometimes. But you know what, it is doable.

Johanne believed that people did not explicitly exercise racism; however, she suggested that there was still racial identification and that it worked subtly. She echoed Sofia and suggested that there was a delicate balance between her identification and her otherness.

Taken together, those who are identified as *different* or *other* believe that they are identified as such because the culture they live in already determines who they are. It is a common understanding that they are playing their difference because they don't want to be isolated due to a cultural struggle. One can challenge his or her discursive position within the hierarchy of privilege as long as he or she is ready for struggle. These accounts suggest that otherness and

Hierarchy of privilege 79

difference can be negotiated to a certain extent; yet, not every individual is ready or willing to negotiate their discursive position.

4.3 Discursive practices of identification and otherness

Any given social institution (e.g., health care systems, prison and correction systems, education and schooling – including online education) represents the institutionalisation of Discourses and discursive practices: it establishes orders of truth and defines what can be accepted as reality in a given society (Foucault, 1978). This perspective provided a conceptual groundwork for many scholars, including educational theorists, working towards equity and social justice. For example, feminist pedagogies have questioned gender roles (Grumet, 1988), post-colonial pedagogies criticised racial and ethnic discrimination (Spivak, 2012), queer pedagogies deconstructed stereotypes of gender performance (Honeychurch, 1996), critical pedagogies examined cultural hegemony (Simon, 1992), and socio-economic, class-based pedagogies critiqued distinction (Aronowitz & Giroux, 1991) when addressing Discourses. It would be erroneous to think online education is exempt from Discourses. Online education, as a type of social institution, is defined by societal Discourses and continues to reproduce them. As I have showed in this chapter, Discourses – discourses of whiteness in particular – delimit people in what they can think, say, or do. Building on that, I exposed how the discursive practices of identification create hierarchies of privilege and position individuals within this hierarchical system.

The first aspect of a discursive regime is that it limits and defines who can speak with what authority. This was particularly evident when individuals I interviewed defined their own hierarchies of privilege. For whites, the hierarchy has two levels: whites are on the top and all the rest are at the bottom. For many students from other racial and ethnic backgrounds, the hierarchy of privilege has three levels: whites are on the top, non-white-Canadians are in the middle, and all the rest are at the bottom. Discursive practices of identification, consequently, create a racial and ethnic taxonomy, by which individuals gain certain levels of privilege and authority.

The second aspect of the discursive regime is that it limits and sets a range of meanings that are available for individuals. This aspect was manifest when individuals were being identified and positioned within the hierarchy of privilege depending on their race, ethnicity, and nationality. In particular, what it means to *be* or *exist* in an online space had different meanings and implications for different individuals. For example, being identified as white means being privileged while other identifications mean being different or diverse. Similarly, for individuals who are identified as white, diversity means opportunities to learn from those who are different, whereas diversity means assimilation and acceptance for individuals who are identified with other racial and ethnic categories.

80 Hierarchy of privilege

The third aspect of the discursive regime is that it limits and imposes specific roles on individuals. This aspect can be seen in how individuals define the ways in which they engage with each other. In particular, different racial, ethnic, and national backgrounds allowed individuals to have different roles and responsibilities. For example, those who are identified as white-Canadians can identify themselves as Canadian while those who are identified as non-white are identified with *hyphened differences* (i.e. Indian-Canadians were more Indian than Canadian or Caribbean-Canadians were more Caribbean than Canadian).

Thus, discursive practices of identification determine three roles for those who are identified as non-white: (1) they should fill less-privileged positions, (2) they should enact their differences, and (3) they should enrich and diversify learning in online spaces. These three aspects are fundamentally dependent upon and related to each other. They determine the manner in which people make sense of their online selves with certain identifications; as online beings with certain rights, roles, needs, and so on. Discursive practices of identification, then, have social and political consequences as they reproduce differentiated power relationships and secure the cultural hegemony of the dominant cultural group. The pedagogical consequences are that while individuals from certain cultural groups are accepted as legitimate participants of a learning community, some individuals are positioned peripherally as they are identified as different or diverse. That is, they are identified in opposition to whiteness; simply put, they are othered.

4.4 Conclusion

In this chapter, I argued that macro-level societal Discourses manifest themselves and affect the ways in which individuals identify themselves in online spaces. I analysed how Discourses of whiteness position individuals within a hierarchy of privilege and determine who has rights, responsibilities, power, and control over others. In particular, I illustrated how students make sense of their online learning experiences with respect to the discursive practices of identification. I sketched how some individuals were able to benefit from the learning community while some individuals were simply othered. This starkly contrasts with the belief that online spaces liberate people from power relations and equalise social status resulting in greater equality of participation.

Being other or different is not inconsequential but rather closely related to how individuals make sense of their experiences. How otherness is enacted and negotiated is explored in depth in the next chapter.

Notes

1 As discussed in Chapter 2, this is a rather normative and essentialist approach that does not explain how discursive practices of identification are defined and shaped with respect to race and ethnicity. My conceptual and analytic approach, therefore, drastically departs from the current understanding in the literature of online education.

Hierarchy of privilege   81

2 His allegory is funny and quite clever as a firewall is software developed for the security of network systems. It controls the incoming and outgoing network traffic by analysing and determining whether data packages are secure or not.

3 As I have articulated in Chapter 2, I acknowledge the digital divide as an important issue regarding digital equity and social justice. However, I am interested in looking beyond the digital divide and investigating what happens after people have access to such digital gadgets or online spaces. For comprehensive analysis of the digital divide with respect to social justice and equity, see Warschauer and Matuchniak (2010).

4 The motivation behind my question is originated in Fanon's (1967) explanation of socio-cultural construction of racial identity and the attendant subjugation determined by the white world. Fanon argues that there is no racial otherness as long as a black person is among blacks. Thus, for Fanon, blacks must be black only in relation to whites. See the chapter called "The Fact of Blackness" in his book *Black Skin, White Masks*.

5 Gulsum points to Islamophobia, a form of prejudice against Muslims. I acknowledge that it is a form of racism and an important issue to be addressed; however, such analysis is beyond the scope of this book.

6 Depending on the audience, subject, and international political climate, Turkey can be associated with both the Middle East and Eastern Europe. Indeed, in our informal and very long conversations, Devran and I talked a lot about Turkey and its dual characteristic as a Middle Eastern and Eastern European country. In this sense, I was expecting Devran to have similar experiences or understanding with Gulsum.

7 The notion of dominant ideology – and ignorance – indeed is very important and a great deal can be said about its effects on equity and social justice. Here, I analyse dominant ideology in terms of diversity; however, I will focus on ideology and explore it in depth with respect to equity and social practices in the following chapter.

8 The relationship between discursive practices of identification and equity is the fundamental motivation behind this research and I will further analyse this relationship in detail later.

9 This is where Foucault departs from classical Marxism. For Marxism, the dialectical relationship between superstructure and base is not subject to change (without revolution) and thus those who are from the ruling class always dominate the subordinate class. For Foucault, power can also be positive. Since power is not monopolised by one centre but distributed among individuals, it is possible to resist against such power structures. However, post-colonial scholarship criticises Foucault's rather optimistic approach. Post-colonial perspectives argue that subordinates and others have no power to struggle.

References

Aronowitz, S., & Giroux, H. A. (1991). *Postmodern education: Politics, culture, and social criticism*. Minneapolis, MN: University of Minnesota Press.

Bannerji, H. (2000). *Dark side of the nation: Essays on multiculturalism, nationalism and gender*. Toronto, ON: Canadian Scholars' Press.

Crenshaw, K. (1989). Demarginalizing the intersection of race and sex: A black feminist critique of antidiscrimination doctrine, feminist theory and antiracist politics. *University of Chicago Legal Forum, 1989*(1), 139–167.

Delgado, R., & Stefancic, J. (2012). *Critical race theory: An introduction* (2nd ed.). New York, NY: New York University Press.

Fanon, F. (1967). *Black skin, white masks* (R. Philcox, Trans., 1st translated ed.). New York, NY: Grove Press.

Foucault, M. (1972). *The archaeology of knowledge and the discourse on language* (A. M. Sheridan-Smith, Trans.). New York, NY: Pantheon.

82 Hierarchy of privilege

Foucault, M. (1978). *The history of sexuality, Vol. 1: An introduction* (R. Hurley, Trans.). New York, NY: Vintage.

Gaztambide-Fernández, R. (2009). *The best of the best: Becoming elite at an American boarding school.* Cambridge, MA: Harvard University Press.

Giroux, H. A. (2011). *On critical pedagogy.* London, UK: Continuum.

Grumet, M. (1988). *Bitter milk: Women and teaching.* Amherst, MA: University of Massachusetts Press.

Hall, S. (2001). Foucault: Power, knowledge and discourse. In M. Wetherell, S. Taylor, & S. J. Yates (Eds.), *Discourse theory and practice: A reader* (pp. 72–81). Thousands Oak, CA: Sage Publications.

Harris, C. I. (1993). Whiteness as property. *Harvard Law Review, 106*(8), 1707–1791. doi: 10.2307/1341787

Honeychurch, K. G. (1996). Researching dissident subjectivities: Queering the grounds of theory and practice. *Harvard Educational Review, 66*(2), 339–356. doi:10.17763/haer. 66.2.322km3320m402551

Mills, C. W. (1998). *Blackness visible: Essays on philosophy and race.* Ithaka, NY: Cornell University Press.

Simon, R. (1992). *Teaching against the grain: Texts for a pedagogy of possibility.* New York, NY: Bergin & Garvey.

Spivak, G. C. (2012). *An aesthetic education in the era of globalization.* Cambridge, MA: Harvard University Press.

Tate, W. F. (1997). Chapter 4: Critical race theory and education: History, theory, and implications. *Review of Research in Education, 22*(1), 195–247. doi:10.3102/0091732x022001195

Warschauer, M., & Matuchniak, T. (2010). New technology and digital worlds: Analyzing evidence of equity in access, use, and outcomes. *Review of Research in Education, 34*(1), 179–225. doi:10.3102/0091732x09349791

Yates, S., & Hiles, D. (2010). Towards a "critical ontology of ourselves"? Foucault, subjectivity and discourse analysis. *Theory & Psychology, 20*(1), 52–75. doi:10.1177/0959354309345647

Chapter 5

Sociocultural production of self

Social presence and social absence

The previous chapter explored how macro-level societal Discourses come into play and affect identification in online education. I drew from Foucault's (1978) definition of discursive practices and explored how Discourses of whiteness delimit the ways in which individuals are identified. I demonstrated that Discourses of whiteness create a hierarchy of privilege and that individuals are identified and positioned within this hierarchy with respect to race, ethnicity, and nationality. In particular, I illustrated that those who are identified as white-Canadians were positioned on top of the hierarchy, whereas those who are identified as non-white were identified as others or different. In this chapter, I built on the notion of *delimitation* and use social presence and social absence to illustrate how difference or otherness is experienced with respect to racial, ethnic, and national identification. Thus, this chapter is concerned with how discursive practices of identification are enacted in online spaces with respect to difference and otherness.

Whiteness studies and post-colonial pedagogies have generally addressed the concept of difference as a marker of identification through which discrimination, oppression, or cultural hegemony is operationalised against those who are identified as non-white (Delgado & Stefancic, 2012). In order to understand how the concept of difference relates to equity and social justice in online education, consequently, I focus on how individuals make sense of their identification as different or other in online spaces. In particular, I analyse what it means to be identified as different or other. I illustrate how difference or otherness is experienced with respect to Discourses of whiteness.

I employ three concepts. The first concept is identification. Since identification refers to how individuals enact within a given context, the concept of identification provides a means to understand how people recreate, adjust, or simply reproduce Discourses. I derive the second concept, social presence, from online education literature. Social presence provides a means to understand how individuals make sense of themselves in relation to those around them (Oztok & Brett, 2011). The third concept is social absence – as I have discussed in Chapter 2, it is built on social presence. Social absence provides a means to understand and address certain identifications that individuals have

84 Sociocultural production of self

but do not necessarily enact in online spaces. Thus, I use both social presence and social absence to understand how individuals experience otherness in an online learning space. By so doing, I address Discourses of whiteness, identification (including social presence and social absence), and otherness as inextricably interwoven.

5.1 Social presence and social absence: I am who I am, or disengagement

Presence and absence are self-referential: they refer to states of being. However, the concepts are considered in relation to reality, truth, and existence in Western thought. For example, in his famous allegory of the cave, Plato pointed out that true being is the ultimate form of presence. Aristotle, on the other hand, set forth the belief that there can be no unmediated forms, but rather being cannot be extracted from representations. With the Enlightenment – particularly with German idealism, the concepts of presence and absence are employed to question the conditions of being. In Being and Time, Heidegger (1962) suggested that presence is precondition for the self. On the contrary, in Being and Nothingness, Sartre (1993) argued that existence is prior to one's presence. That is, individual is born into the material reality of one's body; therefore, one finds oneself inserted into being. With post-structuralism, presence and absence have lost their binary distinction. Deleuze (1990) tried to separate presence from the absolute truth and absence from absolute falsity. Similarly, in *Of Grammatology*, Derrida (1998) criticised the conventional notion that associates existence with presence and suggested a play between presence and absence. In this book, I utilise the idea of the interplay between presence and absence for understanding online selves by arguing that presence is a form of absence and absence can be thought of as a kind of presence. This is where I depart from the conventional online educational research and do not solely depend on social presence but also draw on the concept of social absence for sketching online subjectivities. As I have argued in Chapter 2, online education has accepted presence as the only form of human experience in online spaces. Absence, in this sense, has never been part of the discussion of *being* in online spaces.

Johanne identified herself as a Caribbean-Canadian – as introduced earlier – who was born in a Caribbean country and grew up in Canada. Recall from the previous chapter that she emphasised her "Caribbean identification more so than [her] Canadian identification" because she believed that she was "accepted as Caribbean but not Canadian". Johanne suggested that she is a very active participant who is not shy in bringing her perspectives in discussions. She claimed that, compared to face-to-face courses, she engaged more with her peers: "I talked with my peers, I posted more, I read more, I replied more". Although I cannot validate her participation in face-to-face courses, the log report (automatically collected student data) indicated that Johanne is indeed very active in the online course. She spent 120 hours in aggregate while the

Sociocultural production of self 85

average time spent online per student was 77 hours. Similarly, the number of notes she read and wrote, and the number of replies she received nearly doubled the class average. In a classical sense – that social presence is the degree to which individuals represent themselves – she was socially present in discussions and she said her "social presence represents her Caribbean-self". However, when I asked her if she believes that she truly represented herself she answered with no hesitation:

> No! Although I have always been genuine in my self-representation, I don't truly represent myself. No! And here is why. Ok, for example, they would know which university I got my degrees, they would know what TV shows or music I like. Like, things I shared, you know. They wouldn't know how really I am because there are other aspects of me that I don't talk about. It is only half of me. For example, they wouldn't know what it means to be different because I never talked about it. [. . .] So, . . . so, I think what you present about yourself is only the half of it, right? So, there is always others' assumptions. There is always stereotyping. So, even though I was genuine about myself and my self-representation, I cannot know what others think of me . . . because of um, . . . this . . . stereotypes. And it goes to dominant perspectives, right? So, I cannot know what others get out of me.

Johanne's answer suggested that even though her social presence was a genuine and true representation of herself, there was more to her identification than what she represented. According to Johanne, her online self was "only half of" who she really was. I asked her to explain what was missing in her online self:

MURAT: What was absent in your online representation?
JOHANNE: Well, funny but my ethnicity was definitely absent. I am a Canadian, right? But I was a Caribbean in the [online] course. So, it is funny because I was not a Caribbean-Canadian, but I was simply a Caribbean. So, my ethnicity was not there. You know what I mean?

Johanne's explanation points out how Discourses of whiteness delimit identifications available to individuals. In the online courses I studied, what it means to be Canadian was available to whites. Thus, Johanne believed that she was identified as Caribbean even though she is Canadian. Johanne continued:

JOHANNE: My ethnicity was absent because I didn't even have a chance to bring it in. I wasn't a Canadian whose ethnic background is Caribbean; I was just a Caribbean. So, if I had a chance to be who I was, I would . . . probably use my ethnic background. But, um, now I am . . . not this person, so I don't use my ethnicity. . . . How can I use my ethnicity if I am not using my ethnic background?

MURAT: So, how is your ethnicity absent?

JOHANNE: I am a Canadian-Caribbean. Not just a Caribbean. So, if you make me a Caribbean, you erase my Caribbean-Canadian background. For example, um . . . whiteness defines . . . um, it defines who we are . . . and also it defines who they are; who whites are. So, what I mean by that is that I am a Canadian, but I am accepted as a Caribbean and this is defined by whiteness. Um, so, um, even though I grew up in Canada and I am a Canadian I cannot be a Canadian. So, if I wanted to be a Canadian or accepted as a Canadian I would have to hide my Caribbean background.

Johanne's articulation is quite powerful. She analysed how Discourses of whiteness define what whites and non-white can or cannot claim. Precisely because her Caribbean-Canadian background was "erased", Johanne believed her online self did not represent her. Thus, Johanne's social absence was her ethnic background.

Race, ethnicity, and nationality are common points of juncture between presence and absence for those who were not positioned on top of the hierarchy of privilege. Nalini, who self-identifies as Indian-Canadian, suggested that her ethnicity was absent. I asked her why and she answered:

I don't know. I think it just didn't come up. I mean, I thought it is ok not to mention it. I mean, parts of me were missing. You know, like my culture and cultural background. I could have put more of myself and wrote about myself. But in terms of what I shared with people, I was accurate. But, yes, there were some parts missing. So, I did not reflect myself fully. You know. . . . Honestly, I thought people do not care about it or take that into account; I thought they don't want to know about it. So, um, I thought . . . I thought I should not mention it because I am not a typical Canadian.

Nalini echoed Johanne in many ways. Most importantly, she believed that her ethnicity was absent through being accepted as an Indian rather than an Indian-Canadian. In a preview interview, however, Nalini suggested that she had to be an Indian because it is the role that was expected from her (see previous chapter). Her contradictory explanations suggested that she was caught in a dilemma that she felt her identification as Indian is absent, yet she felt like she is expected to be an Indian. Spivak (2012) calls this dilemma "double-bind"; an irreconcilable binary in which two subject positions can simultaneously oppose yet construct one another. For Nalini, double-bind was the dynamic interplay between Discourses of whiteness and her social absence. In specific, since being intelligent or successful was granted to those who are identified as white (see the previous chapter), Nalini was caught in a double-bind: her ethnic identification on one hand, the risk of being identified as unintelligent on the other. Discourses of whiteness enforce Nalini to be an Indian yet Nalini feels her ethnicity is absent. Thus, for Nalini, similar to Johanne, social presence and social absence were subject to discursive practices of identification.

Sociocultural production of self   87

I wondered what Nalini meant when she said "because I am not a typical Canadian". Nalini explained:

> Well, you have limited social cues in online learning, right? So, people fill in those . . . cues . . . they make guesses . . . um, they stereotype you depending on their dominant ideology. And, they are white. So, let's be honest. They stereotype me depending on what they think of me. . . . They do! They start guessing. [. . .] So, my picture was up there, um, . . . and my name was there, right? So, they guess that . . . um, they assume that I am brown, and I have a different name, so I am not a Canadian or white. (laughs). You know . . . And if you don't represent yourself according to the image they have in [their] mind, they think you are fake.

Nalini's answer typified how Discourses of whiteness manifest themselves in online learning spaces. According to Nalini, people try to make sense of their peers and stereotype each other by using meanings that are defined and delimited by the very same Discourses. This explains why Nalini was caught in a double-bind: she is brown and has a different name; therefore, she cannot be a Canadian, otherwise her peers may think she is "fake". Nalini cannot be an Indian; she must be the Indian her peers assume her to be. Discourses of whiteness not only delimits Nalini's identification (that she is not a Canadian but an Indian) but also determines what it means to be an Indian (that she has to represent herself according to the image her peers have in their minds). Consequently, for Nalini, her social absence was a matter of race, ethnicity, and nationality.

Yet, similarities between Nalini and Johanne were quite interesting. They both believed that their ethnicities were absent from their online selves because they were identified as who they were not: not a Canadian but a Caribbean and an Indian. They both believed that their absence was the direct result of stereotypes that are originated from macro-level societal Discourses.

Being stereotyped in relation to social absence was repeated by Sofia, who self-identifies as Latina. "We all make guesses, right? You start putting stereotypes. You put in dominant ideology", she said. For Sofia, social presence and social absence were matters of identification:

> I think it all comes down to identity and of course because this is [an] online [course], it comes down to social presence, too. Not only your social presence but also your peers', too.

Sofia suggested that social presence – and social absence – is constructed dialogically: one's sense of social presence is not free-floating but is shaped by others' perspectives as well. She continued:

> If you don't have enough [sense of] social presence, you have a disconnection; you, um, you do not learn. And once my experiences, my perspectives,

88 Sociocultural production of self

> or my identity is devalued, then, my social presence . . . um, . . . um, if this is the case, then it is going to break down the communication, break down social presence, and break down the community at large. [. . .] I don't have [sense of] social presence if you don't accept me as I am. I can't be here if you don't accept me as I am.

Sofia's explanation of social presence now shifted from identification to existence. Curious about the interplay between social presence and social absence, I asked her whether she felt absent from discussions:

> Um, I guess I felt so sometimes. I was. . . . Um, I was present, right? I was there, I was participating. And, I was presenting myself; I was presenting my perspectives. But um, . . . I don't know how to explain this. . . . I was sort of experiencing this absence. It wasn't me, fully.

Sofia's answer indicated why identification in online learning spaces should be considered as the dynamic interplay between social presence and social absence. She suggested that she was present and participating in discussions, yet she argued that she felt absent. Since Sofia captured the interplay between the concepts of presence and absence, I introduced to her the concept of social absence (she already knows the concept of social presence through the readings of the course). I was interested in how Sofia thinks of her social absence:

MURAT: So, were there any aspects of you that were absent?

SOFIA: Not that anything was absent per se but I was . . . like I told you, I was considering how much to reveal of myself as opposed to how much to keep it to yourself . . . how much to anonymous. So, there was always . . . a feeling that I was cautious of who I am and how much I contribute. So, what I am trying to say is that, in a general sense, I was absent although I was present. I guess I am confused (laughs). I guess this is what you mean by social absence, right?

Sofia suggested that she was absent from discussions and in this way, she differs from Johanne and Nalini – and from everyone else I interviewed. This finding should be understood with regard to her overall interaction patterns. Sofia was quite vocal and participated in discussions regularly, providing her insights as a teacher. She started her notes with friendly salutes and occasionally used smiley faces – something that indicates high levels of social presence according to current understandings. However, she suggested that she felt she was absent from discussions. She continued:

SOFIA: So, I was absent, and I believe people were filling in my absence with their thoughts and imagination of me. So, this is what I meant [that] your identity is defined for you.[1] And in this case, your social presence is defined for you.

Sociocultural production of self   89

MURAT: What do you mean? Who defines it? How?

SOFIA: Again, it all goes back to . . . ideology, narrative, discourse whatever you want to call it. Every culture has some hegemonic[2] aspects in it. [. . .] And here online, there is this Canadian ideology. Um, in my experience it defines who you can be, online and offline. It does not tolerate or consider other perspectives. That is how cultural hegemony feeds itself into online learning. It is forcing you to be a certain person.

Devran and Gulsum also explained the effects of Discourses on social presence and social absence by means of race, ethnicity, and nationality.

Gulsum, a Canadian born in Egypt who identifies herself as non-white, was not very active in terms of the quantity of notes she posts. She joined in discussions late in the week and she usually logged in to the online space late in the day (she said she is a busy mom of three). She seldom received responses to her notes and did not often receive questions by peers. The log data indicated that she received only 43 replies while the average number of replies received per student was 60. Her reply ratio (correlation between number of replies she received per number of notes she posted) is .47 while the mean reply ratio per a note is .79 for the whole class. I asked her whether she thinks she has a low level of social presence.[3] Gulsum answered that "self-representation cannot be quantified" and added that "numbers do not matter". She suggested that she "must have high social presence" because she "represents [herself] truly". I was curious about what she meant by representing herself truly.

GULSUM: It means that you are not pretending to be someone else. Or it means that you are not trying to fool people or fool yourself by trying to be someone else. You know how people change their identities and act like someone else online?

MURAT: Do you mean something like gender bending or identity bending?

GULSUM: Yes. So, yes, in that sense, I truly represented myself.

Gulsum suggested that her sense of social presence was high because she believed she represents herself online. I asked Gulsum whether she experienced similar challenges in her other courses, whether online or face-to-face. She answered by nodding. I suggested to Gulsum that, according to what she says, her online self also must be immune from racial discrimination.[4] She was confused and surprised with my words:

GULSUM: Um, I never thought about it in that way. [long pause] I guess. . . . Um, I think my online self is actually the um, . . . [my online self] is already the immune version of me. In online, . . . I told you this already, right? . . . I am not bringing in my race or my country of origin. I don't share them. I just hide those things.

MURAT: Hide?

90 Sociocultural production of self

GULSUM: Yeah, hide. You just don't talk about it. And if I don't bring them in, they are not there, right? (laughs)

As the focus of conversation moved from social presence to social absence, Gulsum started to consider the implicit effects of Discourses of whiteness on her online self. I was curious to know more about how she makes sense of her social absence. She suggested that it means she has less to share:

> So, I hide myself and I guess [I] engage less. But I don't mean numbers again. I mean I engage less in a way that um, . . . I am less of me. But again, I am true in a sense that I am who I am but I am. . . . Like I said before, my online self is less of me.

Similar to Nalini, Gulsum believed that she was present because she represents herself, and yet she believed she was absent because she hides herself. Gulsum experienced her social presence and social absence as two contradictory subject positions that simultaneously interact to construct her online self. For Gulsum, presence and absence had an impact on how she engaged with her peers. She said sharing was not an easy process but included some critical decisions because she had to decide how much of herself to reveal. We had the following exchange:

GULSUM: For me to share, um . . . like, I have to be very comfortable and feel safe to share. But you have to work really hard to have that [sense of] comfort within your community. And it is not easy to create that. You have to know that you are not going to be judged or devalued based on your race or any other cultural background. You have to know that . . . you are not accepted as less intelligent because you are Arab or Muslim. You have to know that you are not going to be isolated or left out because who you are. Nobody wants that, right? Um, and it just doesn't happen just like that. Even you try hard; even your instructor or professor try hard, you need time . . . believe me, a lot of time. And you just don't feel comfortable.
MURAT: What if you never feel comfortable?
GULSUM: I don't but this is why I call myself immune from racism. I deal with it.

Despite Gulsum called herself "immune from racism", she did not mean that she was exempt from racism; rather, she meant that she "deal[s] with it". Indeed, Gulsum and all the others identified as non-white argued that they somehow deal with racism. Gulsum's accounts exemplify the idea that race is a problem of non-whites (Crenshaw, 1989). According to this perspective, whiteness is accepted as normative; thus, whiteness is not considered as a racial category whereas all those who are identified as non-white are accepted as racial subjects. My interviews with my participants suggest that social absence is one way to deal with racism in online learning spaces. In specific, individuals' racial or

Sociocultural production of self 91

ethnic backgrounds become their social absence while they are able to present themselves.

I was interested in understanding how Gulsum experiences her social absence:

GULSUM: You just disengage. It is that simple. You become disengaged, and then people think you are just disinterested, or you don't want to participate but you are just disengaged because there is no other way to engage, right? So, what you do is that, you hide yourself and . . . and, um, when you feel comfortable enough, you reveal yourself, you show yourself. And, um, if the reaction [of your peers] is ok; if you feel that it is ok to be yourself, then you are lucky, and you can go ahead. But if not, it is not good, right? You either wait for another moment or just let it go. So, you hide yourself.

MURAT: How do you hide yourself?

GULSUM: When it happens to me, I just superficially engage. I just quote a couple of things from the article and just don't care what others say because it might hurt me. So, you hide yourself because you . . . you want to fit in. It is sort of social sacrifice, in a sense.

I wondered whether Gulsum's meagre amount of participation was related to her social absence. She rejected this idea even before I finished asking the question. Nevertheless, Gulsum suggested that she deals with discourses of identification by disengaging from discussions.

For Devran, an international student from Turkey who identifies herself as white, social absence was "temporal [because] as the course progress, [one] can bring [her] perspectives and experiences". Devran was an active participant and she confirmed that her sense of social presence was high. She believed her social presence is her "accurate and true representation" and she experienced social absence "only for a few weeks at the beginning of the course". She explained:

I wasn't talking much about Turkey at the beginning because I wasn't sure how people would react to that. I guess I was worried that um, . . . I wasn't sure if people would want to listen what I say because I am coming from Turkey and I represent that perspective.

Devran defined her social absence – even though she experienced it only for a short period of time – in terms of nationality. I was curious whether she experienced any racial or ethnic tension with regards to her social presence or social absence. I reminded her of the hierarchy of privilege she suggested[5] and asked her whether she sensed any relationship between such a hierarchy and social absence. She took her time to think before she explained:

Um, I think there must be a relationship; now that I am thinking about it. . . . I mean, again, I was in the middle somewhere [within the hierarchy],

92 Sociocultural production of self

so the perspectives that I didn't bring in, um . . . it might be relatively less significant to those who are [positioned] towards the bottom . . . I guess. . . . So, in theory there must be [a link], but for me it was not that big of a deal. For me, it was my Turkish identity that I didn't . . . use much. But it is ok. But I think for those who are less privileged, it must be harder.

By making a theoretical relationship between hierarchy of privilege and social absence, Devran was able to consider race and ethnicity along with nationality. Despite the fact that she did not experience racial or ethnic social absence, she believed there may be a link as such.

I am curious about what social absence meant for Devran and how she experienced it. She suggested that she had "simply not talked about her Turkish identification as though [she was] not from Turkey". She continued:

but as the course progresses you understand your peers and your peers understand you. They get to know your experiences and your perspectives. And, as the course progress, your peers know that you are coming from a different culture, coming from a different society. So, when you have that, it is ok that you can be yourself. It is only through this understanding. So, you start off as you want to fit in and as the course progresses, you connect with your peers. Then, things change. They change in terms of . . . that . . . um, that you can bring in your actual identity, your actual self. It means that you are more comfortable for bringing in your own identity to the group. . . . It doesn't matter what race or gender or nationality or anything else. And, honestly, if there was not such, um . . . understanding or comfort in group, the whole class would fall apart. [. . .] But there is a comfort level so I was ok.

Devran suggested that she felt comfortable as the course progressed, and consequently she experienced social absence only for a short period of time.

Devran's overall experience suggested that she experienced social absence less overtly compared to those who were identified as non-white. That is, her social absence constituted only one aspect of identification (nationality) as opposed to the combination of three (race, ethnicity, and nationality). For those who were identified as non-white, the implications of social absence are legion:

NALINI: You know, I felt many times . . . um, . . . I was like "don't you think before you talk? You can hurt others' feelings". So when they hurt me; when it happens to me, I filter um, I filter what is coming out from me. I mean, you filter yourself. It happens in face-to-face [courses] and it happens in online courses. It always happens. And it is mean. It hurts. When it happens, even [in] online courses, I do not want to participate anymore. So, I chose not to participate; I chose not to contribute. It broke down my participation and my learning.

SOFIA: I just don't want to participate but I do anyway. I want to wait until I feel comfortable again, but the course is going on and you can't stop posting notes. If I stop participating, I would only punish myself because I can't learn without participating. So, I participate without being myself.

JOHANNE: In my understanding, it is about being. . . . Um, it happens because you just cannot take cultural hegemony out; you just can't. So, there you go, you accept this hegemony or get marginalised. You just can't take hegemony out; it is going to happen. What you do is that you always consider what your position is; you always consider who you are. So, you hide yourself and deal with it. If you need to leave some . . . of your cultural identity out, then you leave it out. You can negotiate it to a certain extent but sometimes you cannot; and you just let it be.

While those who were identified as non-white experience disconnection, those who were identified as white social absence had a different meaning. Discursive practices of identification and hierarchy of privilege seemed to have no significant effect – if any effect at all – on social absence. Rather, social absence was defined in terms of personal traits.

Jeff believed his "online self is just who [he is]" and there was "nothing missing" from his online self. "If anything", he added, "my online self is a politer version of me". He complained that online learning discourse[6] as a writing genre was unnecessarily polite, which according to him "doesn't allow intellectual discussions or fruitful debates but causes rather superficial engagements". Jeff named this genre "politics of politeness":

> After three weeks, I got fed up with that whole online thing. People like "oh, great post! I totally agree with you" or "oh such a fantastic note!" or like "oh thank you so much for your note". All that being nice thing. You know what I mean? I just got really fed up with that. It is like . . . online culture shock.

Jeff believes that "politics of politeness" affects the ways in which people engage with each other. Dissatisfied and displeased, he perceives the implications of such politics as "online cultural shock". I asked Jeff if he experienced or sensed any cultural shock in terms of his race, ethnicity, or nationality. He was negative about my suggestion; however, he acknowledged that "certain individuals from certain cultural groups might feel that way". He added "but I don't know enough about how those people might sense that". Despite Jeff's earlier contention that nothing was missing from his online self, he later suggested that he did give up certain aspects of himself:

> I was asking [myself] "can I fit in while staying true to myself?". I did give up a certain amount of um, . . . I had to give up certain aspects of myself trying to fit in. You just choose not to say those things. But later on, I was like . . . "nah, just I don't care anymore". So, it is the effects of community,

> if you like to say it in that way. It was . . . um, the community was exercising social control over me . . . um, . . . both in good and bad ways. (laughs). Do you know what I mean? It made me, um, . . . more likely to conform to it, in a politer way to say it. I was just being indifferent when I had to conform and when I had to . . . not to say the things I wanted to say.

Jeff experienced social absence with regards to linguistic genre; yet he believed he conformed and gave up certain aspects of himself in order to fit in. For those who were identified as non-white that I interviewed, social absence was a result of otherness and difference, and it caused disengagement. I was curious whether Jeff sensed or experienced it as such. He answered:

> No, I believe it is a personal thing. I just can't stand that language. Um, I am sure others are just fine with it; so, I can't associate it with culture. In terms of disengagement, . . . I wasn't disengaged but I was indifferent. I was like "yeah, whatever".

For Jeff, and others identified as white, social absence was not related to cultural dynamics or Discourses but is largely a personal matter.

Kate, who identifies herself as white, participated in discussions regularly; she posted her notes early in the week. She was quick to reply to those who interacted with her. "I am on top of everything going on in the course [. . .] I am active, I engage, I interact", she said. I asked her whether she was familiar with the concept of social presence. She confirmed that she was. She suggested that her sense of "social presence is really high". She added as she laughs: "I must be overly present if you like to say it in that way". For Kate, her online self was her representation. I asked Kate if there were any aspects of herself that are missing from her online self:

> Um, I am . . . I don't think so. I mean, I believe it is the truest representation of myself. If you ask my peers online who I am, the person they describe is going to be me. But . . . the only thing I can say is that I am a much funnier person in my life. I like to make jokes, especially practical jokes. That's the only thing missing in my online self. I guess I will make more jokes now. (laughs). But, anyway, so my answer is no, there is nothing missing from my online self.

Kate's answer suggested that one of her personal traits – making practical jokes – was absent from her online self and, perhaps, her online self was slightly more serious than who she is. Wondering whether Kate was going to pull any practical jokes on me, I suggested that her online self, according to her explanation, must be "white" since this was how she identifies herself. She replied after she stopped laughing: "yes, I guess so. If I am white, I must be representing white perspectives; so, my online self must be white". I was curious whether Kate would

Sociocultural production of self 95

address her social presence – or absence – as racial or ethnic identification. I asked her what it means to have white social presence and her answer was straightforward: "it means to be me".

Kate's answer pointed out the fact that Discourses of whiteness affect how different individuals experience online learning differently. Identified as white, Kate did not experience any racial or ethnic absence. In other words, Discourses of whiteness were invisible for Kate. She suggested that her "online self must be white". However, as illustrated here, those who were identified as non-white experienced the effects of Discourses of whiteness and "deal[t] with it" through their social absence. Furthermore, Kate's answer suggested that Discourses of whiteness normalise whites and their perspectives as neutral way of being, doing, or saying. Kate did not have to negotiate her social presence or social absence with respect to racial or ethnic dynamics; thus, she suggested that "[her] social presence means to be [herself]". However, as demonstrated above, those who were identified as non-white negotiated their online self (who can be identified as white or Canadian is delimited) and experienced social absence with respect to Discourses of whiteness.

Denise regularly participated in discussions. However, she argued that she "could have participated more but [she] didn't feel connected to her peers much because [she] live[s] at the other end of the world". She said, "you really feel the physical distance even though the Internet allows you to participate from distance". Still, she believed that her "online representation is accurate" and that her peers had "a pretty good sense of [her]". In this sense, Denise suggested that she has a high sense of social presence. I wondered what makes her think that her peers know her well. She answered that she "shares [her] perspectives, so [she] brings in [her] personality"; thus, she suggested "there is nothing [she] hides about [her] personality". I insisted that there may be something that her online peers do not know about her. Denise insisted that she was "pretty honest and open about [herself] and if anything comes up". She continued, she "will bring it up without hesitation". However, she admitted, probably to appease me and change the topic, she did not talk about her hobbies. She asked:

DENISE: Have you heard this famous Latin phrase: Ego sum, qui sum[7]?
MURAT: (I nod)
DENISE: That's exactly what I think of my online self.

It was evident from my conversation with Denise that she denied – or genuinely did not have – any sense or experience of social absence.

Unlike Denise, Amy, Courtney, and Sydney talked about their sense of social absence; however, they addressed it in terms of personal traits or daily life routines. Courtney, for example, did not talk about a certain school she worked at. She explained that "it is extremely insignificant, anyway". Amy teaches English at [a country in Asia]. Her social absence included her "daily life routines that

96 Sociocultural production of self

[she] goes through in [the country she lives]". She added that she did not "want to bother people with her daily life because nobody wants to hear [that]". For Sydney, social absence constituted "obviously, [her] daily life problems, like problems with family or friends". Sydney, however, acknowledged "minorities or under-represented groups might have a different answer for that". I was surprised that Sydney brought up power and Discourses to her explanation. I asked her to articulate more:

SYDNEY: I don't know but it seems to me . . . like those people might have hard, um. . . . It might be hard for them to truly represent themselves because they may not feel comfortable enough.
MURAT: Why they may not be comfortable?
SYDNEY: Well, it is because . . . it is very common that. . . . Ok, so, the course is offered in Canada, right? So, if you are not from this . . . Canadian perspective, then you may not be comfortable enough if you are not coming from that perspective.
MURAT: Why not? What would make them uncomfortable?
SYDNEY: They may feel compelled to . . . present themselves in ways that they . . . in ways that are different from who they are.
MURAT: What do you mean compelled to? Can you explain that?
SYDNEY: Maybe they feel isolated. I am not sure. I mean . . . I don't mean that they don't represent themselves truly. They do. I believe, they do. I am just saying that it may not be as easy for them as it is for me. But this [course] is online, right? So, everybody has more chances. And I believe it is the community that allows that. The instructor established this understanding . . . that um, it is ok to represent yourself. She established that it is ok for everyone to bring their perspectives; it is ok to bring your personality. So, she provided [the understanding] that it is ok to be yourself. Um, it is hard to do it but, um, . . . it is nice that they have that opportunity now.

While Sydney understood her social absence in terms of "daily life problems", she positioned social presence and social absence in relation to discursive practices for those who were identified as different or other. According to her, such discursive practices were manifest in social presence and social absence for "minorities and under-represented groups". Sydney provided a discursive approach to social presence and social absence: that, perhaps, those who were identified as white – those who are on top of the hierarchy of privilege – were exempt from the effects of Discourses. Sydney echoed the online education literature that online context liberates people from social power relations. However, my interviews with those who are identified as non-white suggest otherwise.

Taken together, the discursive practices of identification come into play and affect individuals' online selves. Regardless of their race, ethnicity, or nationality, individuals I interviewed articulated that their social presence represented themselves. For those who were identified as non-white, however, their online self captures only a partial representation of themselves. I argued that social absence can explain how individuals utilise their incomplete selves. Everyone I interviewed, except Denise, provided explanations and examples of their social absence. For those who were identified as white, social absence was a matter of personal story, daily life routine, or personal trait. In their own words, for whites, social absence was not significantly related to their learning. For those identified as non-white, social absence was part of their cultural background: race, ethnicity, or nationality. Such effects can have dramatic outcomes for them, such as isolation, disengagement, or veiled acceptance for the purposes of a parsimonious online experience with peers.

5.2 Discursive subjectivities: know thyself, or stay anonymous

In this section, I utilise and exploit the notion of identification to illustrate how individuals make sense of their online selves. I analyse social presence and social absence as means by which individuals make sense of their online experiences. However, as discussed in Chapter 2, the current literature disregards social absence by equating identification with social presence. According to current perspectives, subject is an autonomous and stable entity, fully endowed with consciousness who is the authentic source of action and meaning. Thus, identification is accepted identically with what has been uttered in online spaces. This perspective, however, not only distinguishes subject from the experience but privileges subject over experience for two reasons: it assumes that (1) an individual is always conscious of himself/herself and (2) that an individual comprehensively understands himself/herself because he/she is the source of the meaning in the first place. On the contrary, Foucault (1978) argues that people operate within the limits of discursive practices; therefore, subjects cannot be fully independent. The notion of discursive practices relocates people from a privileged position to a nexus of subject-power-knowledge.

By conceptualising online selves within this nexus, I address identification as a dialogic construction that is situated within Discourses of whiteness. I focus on the link between social absence and social presence to explore how power, privilege, and hierarchy shape online subjectivities. In particular, I argue that online subjectivities can provide means to understand the hidden curriculum of online education since subjectivity reflects how the curriculum is lived and experienced (Pinar, 2011). By deconstructing online subjectivities, I reconstruct the link between Discourses and equity in online education.

As discussed earlier, Johanne posited that she did not truly represent herself despite her self-representation being genuine. She explained that her representation was half of who she is since her ethnicity was absent from her online self. In order to explain this dilemma (that she is present yet absent at the same time), I used the concept of *double-bind* (Spivak, 2012) to explain how those

98 Sociocultural production of self

who were identified as non-white simultaneously experience two contradictory subject positions. I was curious what social absence (that her ethnicity is absent in her online self) meant for Johanne. She replied:

JOHANNE: It is about. . . . Um, you feel uncomfortable; you feel unease about yourself. It um, frustrates you . . . because you cannot participate or engage because you are not really you.

MURAT: You are not really you? What do you mean by that?

JOHANNE: You are different, right? But I am not different to myself. So, I am this Caribbean person to my peers, but I am a Canadian-Caribbean to myself. So, you play it. Um, play is not the right word, I guess. Let's say . . . um, . . . let's say I don't know. . . .

MURAT: Ok. So, how can you be not you?

JOHANNE: Easy. (laughs). You stay sort of anonymous because it gives you a level of comfort. It makes you feel somewhat comfortable. Let me . . . let me clarify what I mean by that. You are still not yourself, but you feel comfortable enough to participate.

According to Johanne, social absence had direct results on her learning. She claimed that she cannot engage with her friends because she cannot be herself. Staying anonymous was the way to handle such uncomfortable social situations. What did Johanne mean by staying anonymous?

JOHANNE: I use anonymity as a metaphor. Um, I mean it is like being there physically but . . . I mean you can't be there physically in online learning, but you know what I mean, right? So, it is like being there, like being in online discussions but being insignificant at the same time. I think that's what it is.

MURAT: What do you mean?

JOHANNE: It is like being this third person who you are not. [. . .] It is like seeing yourself as two different people. [It is] like being hybrid.

Johanne understood herself as a hybrid person, yet I was not sure whether she referred to the concept of hybrid third person in post-colonial studies. I asked Johanne whether she was familiar with the concept. She said "no" but she added that she may have "a pretty good understanding of the concept without knowing it because this is what [she has] been experiencing". I explained Johanne that in post-colonial research hybridity refers to an *in-between-identity*, in which the coloniser and the colonised are mutually dependent on each other to construct a shared culture (Bhabha, 1994). An in-between-identity has no point of origin or arrival (Ahmed, 2000). Nevertheless, what Johanne explained as *being hybrid* can be best explained through the concept of double-consciousness (Du Bois, 1994), a concept that refers to the notion that black people are able to see racial events from two perspectives. Double-consciousness is understanding the self through the eyes of others; that is, those who are identified as non-white can see themselves through the perspectives of whites. It captures and reflects the ability of non-whites recognising the effects of Discourses of whiteness.

I wondered what this hybrid identification – or double-consciousness – meant to Johanne for her learning. She answers without hesitation:

> Oh, I learn. I do. No problem over there. But it is like you are disappointed because it . . . because you can't stop thinking about that . . . it could have been much better learning experience. You can't stop thinking that you could have said more or done more. For me, it is living with "could haves" or "would haves" (she does quotations marks with her hands).

Johanne suggested that her hybrid identity had very little – if any – effect on learning the subject matter. However, when I asked Johanne to consider the ways in which she engaged with her peers, she explained:

JOHANNE: It definitely contradicts this idea that online learning provides open access.
MURAT: You mean the anytime-anywhere access?
JOHANNE: Yes. Before this online course, I would say yes, online learning supports flexible access. However, I now say no. The reason is that you may be taking the course online and you can, um, actually access it at anywhere at anytime. But at the same time, there are, . . . there are specific discussion habits that are originated from the dominant ideology.

Johanne's explanation is at the heart of this book: having access to online learning does not guarantee equitable learning space since Discourses shape the context, wherein its inhabitants make sense of their daily lives. Johanne pointed out to the fact that dominant ideology, or Discourses of whiteness in this case, shaped how she experienced online learning. She continued:

> You may want to post your thoughts; you may need to respond to a certain individual. But they all are structured and not that flexible when it comes to participation. So, you may access it anytime and anywhere at your own convenience but at the same time you are structured by the dominant ideology, by your peers, and by their frame of mind. So, it means that you have to be very, very, very careful at crafting your answer. You are being this third person, this hybrid person like you said. And if you are not playing by the rules, then you are . . . in trouble (laughs). So, you play by the rule and you are either this hybrid person or you stay anonymous and you participate without any meaning to it. So, either way, your participation is limited.

According to Johanne, Discourses of whiteness determines the ways in which one can be identified in posting or replying to a note. In particular, she said that one had to "play by the rule" and be "very very very careful at crafting [his or her] answer". Thus, Johanne suggested that Discourses of whiteness not only delimit identifications available to individuals but also delimit the ways in which individuals engage with each other. For her, being identified as different meant that her online self was hybrid between who she thought she was and who she was identified as by her peers. Accordingly, Johanne's hybridity limited the ways in which she engaged with her peers: either (1) she had to accept a hybrid identification and be a person who she was not or (2) she denied hybrid identification but stayed anonymous and engaged superficially.

Johanne's explanation of how she experienced her difference revealed the ways in which Discourses of whiteness created differentiated pedagogical implications for those who were identified as non-white. Johanne's experience of the hidden curriculum and her understanding of her difference had many similarities with those who were not positioned on the top of the hierarchy of privilege. In particular, anonymity was commonly associated in my interviews with social absence.

Social absence meant disconnection for Sofia. She believed that she was being stereotyped and that her perspectives were devalued. I asked Sofia whether her sense of social presence had any effect on her learning. Similar to Johanne, Sofia quickly rejected any negative effects. She added: "You can learn. It is not a problem. Everything is online: readings are online, discussion is online. Just log in and read and learn". Sofia's explanations epitomised the online education literature. First, she addressed the curriculum as a matter of subject matter that needs to be transmitted. Second, she suggested that learning is a matter of access to the online space. I reminded Sofia of one of our earlier conversations, where she argued that there is a tension between "how much to reveal of [herself] as opposed to how much to stay anonymous". I suggested for her to consider her previous statement in relation to her participation. Sofia was now able to address the online curriculum as an experience. She articulated how she experienced social absence:

> What it means for participation is a whole other story. It means that you have no choice but follow the path that is already . . . put there for you.

Sofia, similar to Johanne, argued that Discourses of whiteness determined the ways in which people engaged with each other. She continued and explained how Discourses of whiteness affected her identification:

> People had an idea of what it means to be Latina. I mean they think they do but they don't. But they think they do, and they expect you to fit in that image that they have for you. So, this is what I meant by staying anonymous. If you don't fit in that image, you are anonymous.

I was surprised how Sofia and Johanne explained social absence and anonymity very similarly. They both understood their social absence in relation to

Sociocultural production of self 101

who they were not; they both used anonymity to explain how they utilised their social absence. They both had double-consciousness of their identification at the intersection of who they were and who they were accepted as. She continued:

SOFIA: So, anonymity gives you more chances to participate.
MURAT: Interesting. Can you explain to me why or how?
SOFIA: Because if you don't use that anonymity, you can't participate because you can't be someone else. I am not the person [that] they stereotype; I can't be that person. [. . .] So, I stay anonymous when I am stereotyped but still want to participate.
MURAT: So, anonymity is something positive for you?
SOFIA: Um, yes and no. I mean it is not all that positive. I mean, . . . think about it; it is not positive because um, the whole idea of anonymity is bad. So, it is the best you can do.

Sofia's explanation of anonymity was intriguing. For Sofia, anonymity was both positive and negative.[8] In a sense, Sofia had two perspectives on her anonymity: anonymity as an opportunity to participate (positive) and anonymity as being stereotyped as who she was not (negative). I asked Sofia whether she meant both the positive and negative consequences of anonymity in one of our earlier conversations when she said "she was absent although [she] was present". She agreed:

I guess so. I guess you can say that. It means that you can participate without being yourself. It means that you know you are different. And, it doesn't matter how many years you spend here, you will still be that different person because that different person has already been defined; and it never changes. [pause] It means that you are not from here, you are not white or not a Canadian. And, it also means that you can be a Canadian but you can't be white. So, I fit in that definition, so I am accepted as different. This is why I need anonymity.

Sofia's experience of the curriculum suggested that she understood her subjectivity in relation to her social absence and to race and nationality. Accordingly, she understood and accepted that she was different from those who were identified as white. For Sofia, anonymity was the way in which she could participate in and define discussion as a discursive subject.

Nalini's social absence was related to her ethnicity and cultural background. "Parts of me were missing" she said. She reiterated ideology, stereotypes, anonymity, and level of comfort. For Nalini, anonymity could be a good strategy to deal with social absence:

You have a picture and you have a name next to it but at the same time, they are not really seeing you. So, you kind of get to control how you represent yourself online. But online, um, you still have to be careful about what you are saying.

Nalini's explanation revealed an important link between anonymity and Discourses of whiteness. For Nalini, anonymity was a way to "deal with" Discourses of whiteness; that is, a strategy "to control" how to represent herself. Yet, anonymity did not provide a full protection from Discourses whiteness. She continued:

> You have to be careful about yourself and how to present yourself because you will be stereotyped no matter what. So, anonymity can be a good thing because, um, even you have a picture or name, you are still . . . um, you are still not seen. So, you can be more comfortable because it might help you, um. [pause] If you don't want to clash with the ideology, anonymity gives you a certain level of comfort.

For Nalini, similar to Johanne and Sofia, anonymity was double-consciousness: anonymity as an opportunity to have a relative control on her online representation and anonymity as being stereotyped as who she was not.

I was curious about the link that Nalini suggested between ideology, anonymity, and level of comfort. Nalini's answer revealed how Discourses whiteness effected the ways in which she experienced online learning with respect to her *difference*:

> They are linked tightly, I suppose. Here is how I can best describe it. So, ideology sets the tone, right? We are in Canada and we have Canadian ideology. It is about who is a Canadian and who can be a Canadian and who cannot. And it is also about race, and gender, right? And once you have that background understanding, . . . you have certain expectations from people. Like, if you fit in, then you are ok. So, the question is how you can fit in to those expectations. For me, it is through anonymity. I feel um, . . . I fit in when I am anonymous. And it all comes down to the level of comfort. Right? Once you feel you fit in, you are comfortable.

Nalini's approach to her online experience echoed the core themes of this chapter. She situated her online self between ideology – what I call Discourses – on one hand and identification on the other. For Nalini, anonymity was a strategy to control her online representation.

I was interested in understanding how anonymity is related to her participation. She said:

> It means that you accept that some part of yourself is missing; yet you still participate. You can't stop participating because it is the only way you exist in online learning spaces, right? If I don't write anything, there is no Nalini

Sociocultural production of self 103

over there, right? So, I have to . . . so, I keep writing notes and I participate. But sometimes I am there as Nalini, talking about myself and talking about my life and my perspectives and my beliefs and um, I . . . I talk about anything I want to. But sometimes I am not as much Nalini as I want to be. (laughs). I sort of filter out what I write about myself.

Nalini mirrored Johanne and Sofia in her concern that parts of who she wanted to be online were missing. She posited that the quantity of her participation was not affected at all. However, the quality of her participation may be different in that she filtered herself for purposes of anonymity. For Nalini, there was a direct link between her learning process and her social absence. Her final remarks clarified how she makes sense of her online self in relation to her social absence:

NALINI: So, if you look at the course, you will see me there, participating. But if you carefully read it, there are some instances where . . . where I have a few frivolous notes. This is where I was anonymous. I would not participate otherwise. So, what happens is that you end up fitting in at the expense of filtering yourself to an extent. You know what I mean? For me, it was my ethnicity. Like I told you before, I was an Indian, not a Canadian. And that's it. I had no choice; I had no other identity. So, I was being Indian in order to fit in. I can't do anything else, right? So, I guess, um, [. . .] what I can tell is that there were two different Nalini: one was me and the other one was the Indian one. So, my online self was in between those two. Does it make sense?

MURAT: (I just nod)

Nalini defined the dialogic construction of identification. The self is comprised of a multiple consciousness that is shared with others. It is constructed through our personal and social experience (Butler, 1990).

Taken together, accounts provided so far indicate that identification was composed of social presence and social absence in online spaces. That is, identification included not only how individuals represent themselves but also how they do not represent themselves. Social absence had three significant impacts on those who were identified as non-white. First, it affected how those who were identified as non-white make sense of their online selves. In particular, individuals I interviewed articulated that they experienced double-bind (Spivak, 2012) or double-consciousness (Du Bois, 1994) – or *hybridity* in Johanne's own words: the online self is the combination of how they identified themselves as well as whom they were identified. Second, being identified as different led to anonymity. Those who were identified as non-white posited that they stay anonymous when they utilised their difference in discussions. They argued that anonymity gave them opportunities to control their online representation and deal with stereotyping. Third, anonymity led to rather superficial

104 Sociocultural production of self

engagements. Those who were identified as non-white asserted that, when they stayed anonymous, they did not bring in their perspectives and experiences but simply made trivial contributions. Though the impact on participation quantity may not be noticeable, the quality of such engagements may suffer – even though those who were identified as non-white posited that they learned the subject matter. Social absence created differentiated learning experiences, particularly for those who were not positioned on the top of the hierarchy of privilege.

5.3 Conclusion

Identification is an ongoing reconstruction of self; it requires articulation, embodiment, personification, acknowledgement, and engagement. For education, identification includes the ways in which individuals make sense of their pedagogical experiences (Oztok, 2016). Accordingly, I analysed how individuals articulated their own identification in relation to their sense of social presence and social absence.

The findings suggest that while those who are identified as white understand their online self as their social presence, those who are identified as non-white are caught in the double-bind of their social presence and social absence. This means that discursive practices of identification have implications on how individuals experience online learning: those who are identified as non-white understand themselves as cultural others. In other words, non-whites experience the curriculum of online education as cultural others. Cultural otherness is not inconsequential but has implications: it means that non-whites have to use anonymity to handle uncomfortable consequences of being stereotyped. The result of anonymity is not reflected in terms of quantity of participation (notes read and written) but in terms of peripheral and superficial engagement. The findings suggest that discursive practices of identification perpetuate differentiated educational experiences for those who are identified as non-white.

These differentiated learning processes and outcomes for different cultural groups are closely related to and intertwined with macro-level societal Discourses. The next chapter explains such links.

Notes

1 Sofia refers to one of our earlier conversations, which is articulated in the previous chapter.
2 In the next chapter, I will use the concept of cultural hegemony to interpret my findings as evidence of inequity.
3 In a casual exchange before one of our interviews, I explained the concept of social presence when I was briefly explaining my research. Before I asked this question, I made sure Gulsum remembers the concept correctly.
4 When Gulsum and I were talking about her identification, she stated that she is immune from all sorts of racism and discrimination. See the previous chapter.
5 See the previous chapter.

6 Note that he refers to the small d discourses: the linguistic aspects of writing; language-in-use.
7 Verbatim: I am who I am.
8 Similarly, online education literature has long considered anonymity both as positive and negative. As discussed in the Chapter 2, studies that focus on the negative consequences highlight de-individualisation and decontextualisation of learning while studies that focus on the positive consequences underscore the liberating effects of online spaces. Sofia's explanation, however, is drastically different. See Spears and Lea (1994) for more examples.

References

Ahmed, S. (2000). *Strange encounters embodied others in post-coloniality*. New York, NY: Routledge.

Bhabha, H. K. (1994). *The location of culture*. New York, NY: Taylor & Francis.

Butler, J. (1990). *Gender trouble: Feminism and the subversion of identity*. New York, NY: Routledge.

Crenshaw, K. (1989). Demarginalizing the intersection of race and sex: A black feminist critique of antidiscrimination doctrine, feminist theory and antiracist politics. *University of Chicago Legal Forum, 1989*(1), 139–167.

Deleuze, G. (1990). *The logic of sense* (M. Lester, Trans.). New York, NY: Columbia University Press.

Delgado, R., & Stefancic, J. (2012). *Critical race theory: An introduction* (2nd ed.). New York, NY: New York University Press.

Derrida, J. (1998). *Of grammatology* (G. C. Spivak, Trans.). Baltimore, MD: The Johns Hopkins University Press.

Du Bois, W. E. B. (1994). *The souls of black folk*. New York, NY: Dover Publications.

Foucault, M. (1978). *The history of sexuality, Vol. 1: An introduction* (R. Hurley, Trans.). New York, NY: Vintage.

Heidegger, M. (1962). *Being and time* (J. Macquarrie & E. Robinson, Trans.). New York, NY: Harper & Row.

Oztok, M. (2016). Cultural ways of constructing knowledge: The role of identities in online group discussions. *International Journal of Computer-Supported Collaborative Learning, 11*(2), 157–186. doi:10.1007/s11412-016-9233-7

Oztok, M., & Brett, C. (2011). Social presence and online learning: A review of research. *The Journal of Distance Education, 25*(3). Retrieved from www.ijede.ca/index.php/jde/article/view/758/1299

Pinar, W. F. (2011). *The character of curriculum studies: Bildung, currere, and the recurring question of the subject*. New York, NY: Palgrave Macmillan.

Sartre, J.-P. (1993). *Being and nothingness* (H. E. Barnes, Trans.). New York, NY: Washington Square Press.

Spears, R., & Lea, M. (1994). Panacea or panopticon? The hidden power in computer-mediated communication. *Communication Research, 21*(4), 427–459. doi:10.1177/009365094021004001

Spivak, G. C. (2012). *An aesthetic education in the era of globalization*. Cambridge, MA: Harvard University Press.

Chapter 6

Hidden curriculum of online learning

Discourses of whiteness, social absence, and inequity

Lauded by Liberal, Positivist, Determinist, and Fordist perspectives, online education has been promoted as an affordable solution to problems surrounding schooling and public education. Indeed, the literature thoroughly documents that local and federal governments, public school boards, and higher education institutions have been promoting online courses in their commitment to accommodating public needs, widening access to materials, sharing intellectual resources, and reducing costs (Anderson, 2008). Such perspectives contributed to researchers assuming that effective group work and community-building just happen in online courses and that individuals come together as an inclusive group where diversity enriches the learning context. Unfortunately, the same research has largely ignored how such group work may perpetuate inequitable learning situations. In broad outline, I have portrayed the concrete ways in which diversity can also be the very reason that Discourses reproduce unequal learning conditions in online spaces. However, though my work starkly contrasts current understandings in online education literature, this reproduction theory[1] is hardly new (for example, see: Aronowitz & Giroux, 1991; Bernstein, 1977; Young, 1971).

The reproduction theory can be traced back to Durkheim (1956), who argued that social reproduction is an important dynamic to secure the stability (more specifically, the division of labour) of a modern society, in which individuals assume their positions within the social structure. Durkheim suggested that schools provide that stability by socialising individuals into the status quo. Pierre Bourdieu is another important scholar who focused on the concept of cultural reproduction. Bourdieu and Passeron (1990) discussed the role of education in a modern society and argued that the education system was used to reproduce the culture of the dominant class in order for the dominant class to preserve their power. Bourdieu's work was mainly focused on the reproduction of disadvantages and inequalities that are caused by cultural reproduction in schools. According to Bourdieu, inequalities are produced through the education system and other social institutions.

Cultural reproduction theory argues that inequity is reproduced through the existing mechanisms by which continuity of cultural experience is sustained across time: cultural values, practices, beliefs, and norms. In short, inequity is reproduced through Discourses. Educational researchers and scholars have long discussed that Discourses act as an agent of cultural reproduction not through the scientific curriculum, but through the hidden curriculum (Apple, 2004; Giroux, 2011). It is argued that identification is one of the primary means by which cultural reproduction occurs in educational contexts (Holland, Lachicotte, Jr., Skinner, & Cain, 1998). This book follows such an understanding and expands that perspective to describe learning conditions in online spaces.

Cultural reproduction theory provides a simple yet powerful explanation for the unequal distribution of learning opportunities. This book illustrates that, based on their identification, individuals experience differentiated learning conditions and opportunities within an online community. How exactly, then, does identification reproduce inequitable learning conditions? In particular, if – as the literature of online education suggests – the online context is a neutral space, and if anytime-anywhere affordance allows individuals to access the space, what are the ways in which identification reproduces differentiated learning conditions? At the centre of these questions is the cultural explanation of community. I do not regard community as mere communication among participants, where individuals simply learn with and from others. Rather, I accept it as a cultural practice that determines who can speak with what authority, shaping subjectivities by delimiting the positions that individuals can assume. Through the process of identification, therefore, individuals understand their difference and behave accordingly within their community. And, through this cultural reproduction, inequity seems natural and inevitable.

In what follows, I shall draw on the analysis in the previous chapters and explain in detail how discourses of identification operate to produce inequitable learning experiences.

6.1 Neutral space, or material realities: online self

Understanding how the online context is formed and how identities are created are the preliminary steps towards understanding the discourses of identification. This understanding necessarily depends on conceptualising the online context as a terrain of cultural and political struggle. It depends on addressing the context as a dynamic place, where daily life materiality is manifested in online selves. In online spaces, daily life manifests itself through construction and enactments online selves.

Writing oneself into an online being can be quite challenging. It involves more than writing a few words and pairing that text with a picture. It is a negotiation of the self. Thus, much consideration and thought can be involved in how to present oneself. "It is just like you are introducing yourself for the first time . . . [and] it is your personality that you have to keep up to the end of the course", Johanne said. Presenting one's online self is tantamount to being alive in online learning spaces; it allows people to embody their online existence and create their online selves, filling the absence left by physical bodies.

When people create their online selves, they do not create a personality that is wholly different from who they are or what they do in their daily lives; rather, they reproduce themselves in a digital space. They derive from the very same material and symbolic resources in which their daily life is situated. Courtney said, "I am who I am, and my online self is the same". Similarly, Sydney articulated that she wanted to be known as who she actually is: "I wanted them to get a general sense of who I am . . . like . . . like they would know me in a face-to-face space". Through online selves, therefore, the online context becomes embodied, where the social, political, economic, and historical dynamics of the broader society is reproduced. Indeed, as Johanne suggested, online selves set the tone for the context, as well as for individuals: they define who one is, is going to be, and wants to be in an online space.

Once the context is socially constructed, individuals negotiate their identifications and try to impress each other in order to portray themselves as good students. What it means to be a good student is not an open-ended question but is defined by Discourses of whiteness: being a good student is a white property. Those who are identified as white are accepted as intelligent and successful while those who are identified as non-white have to convey the impression that they are as good, as intelligent, as successful, and as desirable as whites are believed to be. Therefore, by highlighting their achievements, traits, desires, hobbies, and qualities in their profile pages, the participants reproduce their online selves in line with the white norms of beauty and intelligence. This does not mean that non-white people are unintelligent or undesirable nor does it mean that they want to be seen as white. Rather, it means that by highlighting their achievements and success in line with the Discourses of whiteness, those who are identified as non-white try to claim their legitimacy, their right to be in the online course. Through impression management, those who are identified as non-white negotiate their status of belonging to their community.

Online selves are created through what Butler (1990) calls performative repetitions: cultural construction of self through the repetition of performances. The performing online self not only embodies people in an online context but also situates and contextualises them in relation to those around them. Therefore, the performance of self in online spaces reproduces macro-level societal Discourses – Discourses of whiteness to be precise – under which people perform what it means to be *a good student*.

6.2 Open-flexible access, or Discourses of identification: difference and otherness

The nexus between macro-level societal Discourses and identification constitutes the meanings that are available and the roles that can be assumed. It determines what one can think, say, and do in a given context (Foucault, 1972, 1978). Thus, the outcomes of discursive practices can never be equal or neutral. In other words, different individuals experience discursive practices differently at any given time, and the implications of those discursive practices necessarily vary as well. In the online courses I studied, discursive practices of identification create a hierarchy of privilege.

Discursive identification, then, determines how individuals are positioned in relation to each other. Regarded as white property, intelligence, privilege, and positive discrimination are given to those that are identified as white. For example, Denise, who identifies herself as white anglophone, argued that "certain people are entitled for certain privileges" and she added that her "privilege is based on [her] cultural background, particularly [her] ethnicity". Jeff, who identifies as white, articulated that his race and ethnicity afford him positive discrimination. Privilege, then, is granted to those who are identified as white; thus, power and status quo are racialised. In other words, privilege is equated with being white. Such discursive identification has direct consequences for how both whites and non-whites are positioned in relation to each other: those who are identified as white are on the top of the hierarchy and those who are identified as "non-white and all the others and immigrants" – as Denise put it – are somehow positioned below. Discursive practices of identification, therefore, enforce an implicit understanding that those who are not on the top of the hierarchy of privilege are somehow different. In other words, while those who are identified as white are accepted as neutral Canadians, those who are identified as non-white are accepted as different or other.

Diversity is a central concept for understanding how difference or otherness is understood and utilised. Talking about diversity as a personal difference allows white people to disregard discursive practices that preserve their status quo within such diverse groups. For those who are identified as white, diversity means different perspectives that non-white people bring to discussion, as Kate put it. For those who are identified as non-white, however, diversity means "the perspectives and experiences that [they] bring in". As Nalini, a second generation Canadian who identifies herself as Indian-Canadian, said, it is her role to enrich and diversify the process of learning. Discursive practices of identification, then, determine the role that those who are identified as non-white are supposed to assume within the hierarchy of privilege: they are the curriculum from which others can learn (Gaztambide-Fernández, 2009). In other words, regarded as a white property, being a neutral Canadian is associated with those who are identified as white. Thus, the roles for non-whites are determined by Discourses of whiteness: those who are identified as non-white are supposed to *enrich* the discussion and *diversify* white people's learning experiences.

Taken together, those who are identified as different or other believe that they are identified as such because the culture they live in predetermines how

110   Hidden curriculum of online learning

they can be identified. It is a common understanding that those who are identified as non-White are displaying their difference because they don't want to be isolated due to a cultural struggle.

6.3 Equality or equity: rules of engagement

Being identified as other or different is closely related to how individuals make sense of their online experiences. Considered in terms of educational equity, how otherness is enacted, negotiated, and valued is important for understanding the difference between equality and equity. As I have argued in Chapter 2, equality refers to comparisons of quantity while equity is concerned with subjective quality. Thus, how individuals make sense of their otherness or difference can explain how identification can create inequitable learning context even when the quantity of participation is relatively equal among individuals. In order to address identification as a dialogic construction, I conceptualise online selves as inextricably interwoven between social presence and social absence. That is, one's online self relates not only to how individuals represent themselves but also to how they do not represent themselves.

For those who are identified as white, identification and hierarchy of privilege seem to have no significant effect – if any – on their social absence. For them, social absence is defined in terms of personal traits. For those who are identified as non-white, however, social absence has a different meaning; their social absence is part of their cultural background: race, ethnicity, or nationality. For example, Johanne posited that she did not believe she represented herself truly since her ethnicity was absent. She argued that her online self is only half of herself. Thus, for those who are identified as non-white, social absence is the means by which they are identified as different from whites. Being caught in white interpretative lenses, those who are identified as non-white experience their online selves from two oppositional subject positions. They experience their social presence and social absence as two contradictory subject positions that simultaneously interact to construct their online selves. In other words, their online self is a double-bind (Spivak, 2012).

In order to "deal with" this double-bind, those who are identified as non-white have to negotiate their online selves with respect to Discourses of whiteness. For those who are identified as non-white, identification is a tension between stereotypes on one hand and anonymity on the other. In either case, those who are identified as non-white have to identify themselves as who they are not when they engage with their peers. For example, Gulsum postulated that she cannot share much with her peers because she hides her race, faith, and country of origin. As Johanne said, those who are identified as non-white have to "play by the rule" and be "very very very careful" with negotiating their social presence and social absence. Such negotiation has dramatic outcomes, including isolation, disengagement, or veiled acceptance for the purposes of a parsimonious online experience with peers. Consequently, the tension between

Hidden curriculum of online learning 111

stereotypes and anonymity is a delicate balance that those who are identified as non-white have to figure out in order to claim their right to be included in the online learning community.

Deconstructing lived experiences and identification reconstructs the link between Discourses of whiteness and equity in online education. One way to understand this link is through an appreciation of how social presence and social absence are racialised with respect to Discourses of whiteness. In particular, being a good, successful, intelligent, desirable, and deserving student is reproduced in online learning spaces through the racialised understanding of social presence and social absence. Thus, social presence and social absence not only secure the property of whites but also reproduce the colonial and white-supremacist understanding of Canada as an imagined nation of whites.

6.4 Cultural hegemony: unequal learning context

Hegemony refers to dominance, especially by one state or social group over others. Hegemony, particularly cultural hegemony, is associated with the work of Marxist philosopher Antonio Gramsci, who refused to separate culture from power, knowledge, and identities. Gramsci (2000) redefined how politics bore down on everyday life through its pedagogical practices, suggesting that hegemony is retained primarily through culture as the subordinate groups adopt the dominant group's values, beliefs, and perspectives. According to this perspective, Discourses are natural and thus have a powerful impact on shaping everyday interactions. For Gramsci, cultural hegemony is achieved when subordinates take daily inequities for granted and as such think and act in ways that are consistent with the status quo. It is through normalisation and acceptance that hegemony is reproduced. Gramsci's work provides a theoretical framework for understanding how hegemony is experienced and in return reproduced through schooling and public education.

In the field of education, cultural hegemony refers to the idea that curriculum is not neutral but serves the interests of one social group over the others; in particular, it conveys white, male, middle-class, and heterosexual world views (Baszile, 2010). With the re-conceptualist[2] movement, the concept of the hidden curriculum is widely used to explain the reproduction of cultural hegemony and social inequity (see, for example, Apple, 2004; Pinar, 2011). The hidden curriculum subtly (through students' day-to-day experience of social life) yet deliberately (through policy makers at school boards or at local and federal governments) maintains the dominant groups' privilege and creates inequity that is based upon cultural differences (Aronowitz & Giroux, 1991).

The relationship between hidden curriculum and the concept of difference is at the centre of many theoretical and pedagogical approaches that work towards equity and social justice. Yet, online education research has idealised the concept of cultural difference and narrowly addressed it for the sake of promoting its liberal, positivist, Fordist, and determinist perspectives. In order to understand equity and social justice in online education, Discourses of whiteness must be addressed within and through power relations. To this end, in this book, I illustrated how the hidden curriculum of online education maintains cultural hegemony and creates an inequitable learning context through cultural differences. When equity is considered as a more fair learning context, identification becomes means by which the hidden curriculum operates to produce inequitable learning experiences. In particular, individuals experience differentiated, and unequal online learning conditions based on their identification. Macro-level societal Discourses – precisely, Discourses of whiteness – manifest themselves within online spaces through online selves (Chapter 3). Online selves create a discursive space, in which individuals are positioned within a hierarchical system based on their identification (Chapter 4). Identified as different or other, those who are identified as non-white experience the "double-bind", resulting in superficial or peripheral engagements (Chapter 5).

Many students continue to experience inequity through the digital divide. Yet, educational inequity still exists even when one has crossed the digital divide and has access to digital resources. Access does not solve nor provide equitable learning conditions. Equity is a continuous process that requires awareness of the material realities of students with different cultural backgrounds, as well as a commitment to solidarity through diversity and difference.

6.5 Last words: conclusion, limitations, and future studies

In this book, I illustrated how students experience the curriculum of online education with respect to issues of equity and social justice. I defined equity as the fair distribution of opportunities to learn within a fairer learning context, and analysed how the hidden curriculum of online education maintains cultural hegemony and creates inequitable or unfair learning experiences through cultural differences. I argued that such inequitable learning experiences are not random acts but rather represent the existing inequities in society at large through cultural reproduction.

A major goal of this book is to challenge the current understandings of equity in the field of online education and illustrate how and in what ways inequitable learning experiences can occur in online education. I hope that this book will provide inspiration to further expand the literature of online education by sparking thought, controversy, debate, and further research on this topic.

Notes

1 Social – or cultural – reproduction theory argues that schools are not institutions of equal opportunity but mechanisms for perpetuating social inequalities to preserve dominant cultural groups' advantage (Apple, 2004).

2 The re-conceptualist movement understands the school curriculum as a form of political praxis. Its aim is to understand, not just implement or evaluate, the curriculum.

References

Anderson, T. (2008). Towards a theory of online learning. In T. Anderson (Ed.), *The theory and practice of online learning* (2nd ed., pp. 45–74). Edmonton, AB: Au Press.

Apple, M. W. (2004). *Ideology and curriculum* (3rd ed.). Boston, MA: Routledge & Kegan Paul.

Aronowitz, S., & Giroux, H. A. (1991). *Postmodern education: Politics, culture, and social criticism*. Minneapolis, MN: University of Minnesota Press.

Baszile, D. T. (2010). Hegemony. In C. Kridel (Ed.), *Encyclopedia of curriculum studies* (pp. 432–433). Thousands Oak, CA: Sage Publications.

Bernstein, B. B. (1977). *Class codes and control: Towards a theory of educational transmissions* (Vol. 3). London, UK: Routledge & Kegan Paul.

Bourdieu, P., & Passeron, J.-C. (1990). *Reproduction in education, society and culture*. Thousands Oak, CA: Sage Publications.

Butler, J. (1990). *Gender trouble: Feminism and the subversion of identity*. New York, NY: Routledge.

Durkheim, É. (1956). *Education and sociology*. New York, NY: Free Press.

Foucault, M. (1972). *The archaeology of knowledge and the discourse on language* (A. M. Sheridan-Smith, Trans.). New York, NY: Pantheon.

Foucault, M. (1978). *The history of sexuality, Vol. 1: An introduction* (R. Hurley, Trans.). New York, NY: Vintage.

Gaztambide-Fernández, R. (2009). *The best of the best: Becoming elite at an American boarding school*. Cambridge, MA: Harvard University Press.

Giroux, H. A. (2011). *On critical pedagogy*. London, UK: Continuum.

Gramsci, A. (2000). *An Antonio Gramsci reader: Selected writings 1916–1935* (D. Forgacs, Ed.). New York, NY: Schocken Books.

Holland, D., Lachicotte, Jr., W., Skinner, D., & Cain, C. (1998). *Identity and agency in cultural worlds*. Cambridge, MA: Harvard University Press.

Pinar, W. F. (2011). *The character of curriculum studies: Bildung, currere, and the recurring question of the subject*. New York, NY: Palgrave Macmillan.

Spivak, G. C. (2012). *An aesthetic education in the era of globalization*. Cambridge, MA: Harvard University Press.

Young, M. F. D. (1971). *Knowledge and control: New directions in the sociology of education*. London, UK: Palgrave Macmillan.I

Index

agency ix, 5, 8, 22

class 9, 10, 21, 30, 35, 38–39, 47–48, 57–60, 62, 66, 79, 81, 85, 89, 92, 106, 111
community/ies 1, 6, 10, 12–13, 16, 19–21, 25–27, 30, 33, 37, 49, 51–52, 54, 69, 72, 77, 80, 88, 90, 94, 96, 106–108, 111
culture 4–5, 10, 14, 26, 29, 33–34, 61, 71, 73–75, 77–78, 86, 89, 92–94, 98, 106, 109, 111
curriculum x, 1–5, 9, 13, 40, 57, 71–73, 75, 97, 100–101, 104, 107–111

difference 7, 9–12, 17, 20, 24–26, 33, 53–54, 67, 70, 72–75, 77–80, 83, 94, 100, 102–103, 107–111
discursive regime 53–55, 58, 79–80
diversity viii, x, 11–12, 57–58, 69–75, 79, 81, 106, 109
double-bind 86–87, 97, 103–104, 110

economic ix, 2, 4–5, 7–8, 13, 17–19, 24, 33, 51, 58, 63, 70, 79, 108
ethnic(ity) 9, 30, 39, 51, 58–59, 61–72, 78–80, 83, 85–87, 89, 91–93, 95–98, 101, 103, 109–110

gender 2, 9–10, 21, 23, 26, 53–54, 57, 60–62, 71, 79, 89, 92, 105

hegemony viii, x, 2, 11, 19, 22, 25, 27, 33, 79–80, 83, 89, 93, 104, 111–112
hierarchy x, 12, 53, 57–83, 86, 91–93, 96–97, 100, 104, 109–110

identification 2, 7–10, 12, 19, 21–28, 30, 32–33, 37–38, 49, 51, 57–58, 61, 64–69, 71, 72, 75–81, 83–88, 91–93, 95–97, 99–104, 107–111
identity/ies ix, 3, 9, 12, 14–15, 18–21, 23, 28, 32, 34, 38, 53–54, 57, 69, 71–72, 76–77, 81, 87–89, 92–93, 98–99, 103, 111
impression management x, 22, 24–25, 37, 39, 44–46, 49–53, 108
isolation 1, 23–24, 41, 76–78, 90, 96–97, 110

marginalisation x, 1, 7, 10, 19, 33, 93
multicultural(ism) viii, 11–12, 72

normalisation 9, 11, 59, 61, 95, 111

online self 23–26, 30, 37–44, 47, 50, 53, 77, 85–86, 89–90, 93–95, 97–98, 100, 102–104, 107–108, 110
otherness 7, 12, 57, 76–81, 83–84, 94, 104, 108–110

political ix, 2–5, 8, 11–13, 17–19, 24, 27, 29, 32–33, 38–39, 51, 54, 59–60, 65, 70, 74, 80–81, 107–108, 113
postcolonial viii, ix, 28, 33, 60, 79, 81, 83, 98, 105
power ix, 4–5, 7, 9, 11, 13–14, 19, 27, 32–33, 44, 54, 58, 61–63, 68, 75–76, 80–81, 86, 96–97, 106–107, 109, 111–112
privilege vii, 7, 51, 57–69, 71–80, 83, 86, 91–93, 96–97, 100, 104, 109–111

race x, 2–4, 9–10, 21, 23, 25, 29–30, 39, 57–69, 71, 78–80, 83, 86–87, 89–90, 92–93, 96–97, 101–102, 106, 109–110
representation 23, 25, 33, 37–38, 44, 50, 53, 85, 89, 91, 94–95, 97, 102–103
reproduction 4, 18–19, 58, 106–107, 111–112

social absence 24–27, 77, 83–84, 86–98, 100–101, 103–104, 110–111

social justice ix, x, 6, 22, 28–30, 62, 79, 81, 83, 111–112

social presence 1, 24–27, 77, 83–91, 95–97, 100, 103–104, 110–111

technology 2–9, 13, 22–23, 33, 40–41, 49, 63

whiteness viii, ix, 12, 14, 27, 32, 39, 50–54, 57–62, 64–66, 68–69, 71, 74, 77–80, 83–87, 90, 95, 97, 99–100, 102, 106, 108–112

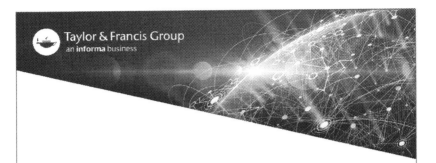

Printed in the United States
by Baker & Taylor Publisher Services